Poems from the Río Grande

CHICANA & CHICANO VISIONS OF THE AMÉRICAS

Poems from the Río Grande

RUDOLFO ANAYA

Foreword by
Robert Con Davis-Undiano

UNIVERSITY OF OKLAHOMA PRESS : NORMAN

LIBRARY OF CONGRESS CATALOGING-IN-PUBLICATION DATA
Anaya, Rudolfo A.
  [Poems. Selections]
  Poems from the Río Grande / Rudolfo Anaya ; foreword by Robert Con
Davis-Undiano.
     pages cm. — (Chicana & Chicano Visions of the Américas ; Volume 14)
     ISBN 978-0-8061-4866-3 (pbk. : alk. paper)
     I. Title.
     PS3551.N27A6 2015
     811'.54—dc23
                              2015003803

Poems from the Río Grande is Volume 14 in the Chicana & Chicano Visions of
the Américas series.

The paper in this book meets the guidelines for permanence and durability of
the Committee on Production Guidelines for Book Longevity of the Council on
Library Resources, Inc. ∞

1 2 3 4 5 6 7 8 9 10

With love for Patricia. We had such wonderful times on this earth, so many good memories. I thank my parents for the values they taught me, and I thank my fellow Nuevo Mexicanos, whose stories and songs daily inspire my poetic soul. New México is a special place; let us take care of the land and its rivers. As long as we are in tune with the spirits of this place, we will prosper. To my readers I wish good health and joy. Open up your hearts and let love come in.

CONTENTS

SERIES EDITOR'S FOREWORD

The University of Oklahoma Press is proud to present *Poems from the Río Grande*—the latest offering by Rudolfo Anaya in the Chicana & Chicano Visions of the Américas book series. For the first time, Anaya's current and future readers will be able to enjoy his poetry in one volume—the definitive text of the twenty-eight poems that Anaya judges to be his best or most interesting poems to date. Presented here with the author's general introduction, this collection will be of interest to scholars, but also to students and general readers who want access to Anaya's poetry as a single body of work.

Anaya was born in 1937 in the village of Pastura, New Mexico, near the small town of Santa Rosa. His family soon moved to Santa Rosa and then in 1952 to Albuquerque, where he attended the University of New Mexico, earning master's degrees in literature and counseling. He taught in the Albuquerque public schools and at the University of New Mexico, where he is now professor emeritus in the Department of English Language and Literature. A major writer of the twentieth and twenty-first centuries, a storyteller and poet who many believe is one of the best writers in America, Anaya is credited with being the "godfather" of the Chicano (Mexican American) Renaissance in the early 1970s. He also remains the novelist most widely read in the Chicano community. One of the most respected of living American writers, Anaya has done much to bring worldwide recognition to Chicano literature and culture. Owing to the continuing appreciation of his work and his generosity to young authors, he continues to be an inspiration to countless Latino and Latina writers, as well as a towering figure for a large reading public.

Known primarily as a novelist, Anaya has been widely praised for his poems, which have been published individually across the United States and around the world. They reflect many aspects of Mexican American and Latino culture and contemporary American society. Mexican American readers will see themselves in and be inspired by Anaya's poetry. General readers will be enlightened by his insightful views and explorations of Mexican American culture. All readers will be immediately drawn to "A Child's Christmas in New Mexico," "Song to the Río Grande," "Walt Whitman Strides the Llano of New

Mexico," and "Isis in the Heart: A Love Poem for Patricia." These poems, along with "Ismith Khan in the Jemez Mountains," "The Adventures of Juan Chicaspatas," and "Sailing to Barcelona," focus on dramatic moments in which tradition and contemporary culture collide and on how the rise of the Latino community impacts and subtly enriches what it means to be an "American." Addressing these and other issues, Anaya explores modern values and beliefs with great insight and timeliness.

The poems collected here also have the same clarity of presentation that readers appreciate in Anaya's fictional depictions of Mexican American and Southwest culture. In "A Child's Christmas in New Mexico," in particular, there is a crystalline vision of nature's promise of renewal, the snow-covered plain in eastern New Mexico when, on "Christmas morning," a "silent winter storm has swept / across the llano." On this morning, Anaya discovers anew the presence of La Llorona (the folkloric figure of the crying woman), Buddha, Muhammad, and Christ. There may be no better evocation of the subtle mixing of different cultures and a mestizo sensibility in the Southwest than this poem's description of how, through these various traditions and in relation to these religious figures, "we are reborn cada día / until the world's end." All of these poems ring true with a wonderful, clear voice. In them, Anaya is at full power as the poet of the llano, the writer who sees the modern world reflected in the microcosm of the landscape surrounding the small villages of eastern New Mexico.

Anaya's poetry is elegant in its intensity and in its wide-ranging treatment of the myths of the Southwest, Mexican American folklore, the legacy of César Chávez, Christmas traditions in New Mexico, and the Egyptian myth of Isis and Osiris transplanted to the Southwest, among others. Whereas his novels and plays deal with the furthest reach of issues relating to life in the Américas, contemporary values, and directions in contemporary culture, the poems focus on similar issues on a smaller scale, and sometimes under a microscope, in ways that will be even more accessible to a great many readers. The perspectives of this versatile poet and shrewd observer of modern culture and society will provide meaningful insights into many issues and trends in contemporary culture.

Teachers of Chicano studies will now have available Anaya's poetry for courses, and since poetry as a form is eminently teachable, many students and general readers will now discover this major author for the first time. His many books—including *Bless Me,*

Ultima; *The Silence of the Llano*; *Shaman Winter*; *The Man Who Could Fly and Other Stories*; and *The Essays*—have reached millions of readers. Anaya's poetry, like his novels, is not intended merely for scholars, libraries, and classrooms, but is there for all who care about the significance of tradition and a sense of place and culture in modern literature.

Anaya's poems are filled with childhood images and memories of the New Mexico *llano* (plains), *gente* (people), tragedies, triumphs, and the Spanish/mestizo culture unique to New Mexico. Out of these childhood experiences, he forges the themes of his writing, as clearly seen in his award-winning novels such as *Bless Me, Ultima* (1972), *Tortuga* (1979), and *Alburquerque* (1992). At the heart of these works is a closely watched encounter between everyday life and the world of ritual. He wants literature and myth to work together to bring people to attention regarding what matters most in their lives—the sacredness of land, tradition, and the healing potential of culture itself.

In the twenty-first-century world of rapid change, political instability, environmental crises, and instant communication that can also distract and displace, ecofeminist Vandana Shiva offers that only by "rooting identity in a 'sense of place'" can communities deepen and make more effective their understanding of issues relating to "gender, class, ethnicity and other constructions of difference, identity politics, and the environmental movement."[1] This is Anaya's vision, too, suggesting that all communities are enriched spiritually when they are grounded by ties to land and culture, and thus are better able to navigate the complex modern world. His poetry teaches about the need to reconnect to land, tradition, and community in order to remember the why, what, and who of the human adventure. Above all else, it offers a fuller grasp of life in the twenty-first century and the demands that the modern world makes on those trying to understand it.

The poems in this volume gaze outward toward the past of the Américas and inward toward that past's persistence in New Mexican culture and landscape. Celebrating the cultural and spiritual life where all are "reborn cada día / until the world's end," the poems search for the living dimension of land and culture and the potential for discovery. If these poems from the Río Grande seem to regard New Mexico and the Southwest as sacred places, it is because so many people have journeyed there in search of truth. Anaya counsels the urgency of learning from land and landscape's spiritual dimension. Enacting a kind of spiritual truth and reconciliation and demonstrating an openness to what will yet emerge from the New

Mexican landscape, these poems ask readers to awaken to the truths that are becoming available, as Anaya comments in *Shaman Winter*, in order to help "the human dream" in the Américas to be "born again." Asking for vigilance and willing participation—and, above all, focused attention—Anaya asks readers to author their own narratives and to be alive to the cultural and spiritual possibilities that are always on the verge, if they will only be attentive, of opening before them.

Rudolfo Anaya is one of the important writers of the modern era, and the publication of this book, the sixth volume of Anaya's work to be published by the University of Oklahoma Press, constitutes an important contribution to Mexican American culture and the flourishing of Chicano poetry.

ROBERT CON DAVIS-UNDIANO

1. Vandana Shiva, "Subversive Kin: A Politics of Diversity," in *Chicano Culture, Ecology, Politics: Subversive Kin*, edited by Devon G. Peña (Tucson: University of Arizona Press, 1998), viii.

PREFACE
Poetry as Ritual

Soon after I published *Bless Me, Ultima,* readers told me they found lyrical passages in the novel. So even in prose, something of my poetic voice was shining through, a sensibility I acquired as a child listening to New Mexican songs and folktales recited by elders from my community. Other rhythms filled my growing-up years: the song of the Pecos River, where I played; the wind's melody in cottonwood trees; voices whispering across the llano; owls and coyotes calling; mockingbird chatter; the warble of meadowlarks; the plática of the women who visited my mother, and of my abuelo and my tíos discussing work on the acequia and their farms in the Puerto de Luna Valley; the stories neighbors brought into our home. Even the imaginative stories my schoolyard friends told were mythopoeic.

The list of voices goes on and on, as do the memories.

I loved listening to cuentos, the Hispanic folktales that catapulted me out of my world and into the magical time that stories create. But the world that a story creates is temporal. No matter how enchanting and captivating a story is, when it ends one returns to reality, perhaps a bit wiser. As I grew older, I began to understand that stories and poems are a form of ritual. Rituals, as they are practiced in older traditional cultures, transport the self into the Time of the Gods, a view of the Absolute. Stories and poems cast the self into the truth beyond reality, and as such they are ritualistic. When one participates fully in a story or poem, one catches a glimpse of Truth, and when the story ends, one returns fulfilled to one's community.

As a child I felt that sense of being cast out of self when I listened to stories. For the first seven years of my life, the stories and songs I heard were recited in New Mexican Spanish, the oral tradition that nurtured me. Those wonderful storytellers knew how to make a story come alive; they knew how to transport a child into the world of imagination.

My Nuevo Mexicano community is heir to a large storehouse of cuentos and songs, and by passing this legacy from one generation to the next, we have preserved our poetic and cultural heritage. Those stories were my initiation into the transforming world of story. I know

now that the elders were molding me into a future storyteller. The New Mexican curanderas—women healers—I knew cared for the spiritual health of the community; our storytellers did the same. Both were involved in rituals that transformed profane time into sacred time, a healing time for the soul. So those wise people were my first guides into the world of ritual.

At school I discovered that books created the same magic I felt when listening to stories in the oral tradition. Reading cast me into the story, too. The comic book stories that friends shared with me had the same power. Later, when I watched 1940s movies in our hometown theater, I felt enthralled as I entered the story on the screen. When I recited the catechism with my mother, the sing-song questions and answers cast me into an awareness of God. It seemed the world around me was full of stories, and the incredible gift latent in stories was, again, the building of soul, the healing that came to the soul. I began to understand that stories and poems in all their forms were healing rituals.

Prose and poetry are not distant cousins; they often walk hand in hand. Poetry is embedded in story. The first poems I heard were Spanish rhythms used by New Mexican storytellers. I also listened closely to the cadences in my mother's prayers. Reciting the rosary was moving through mysteries, a long story with cleansing power in its recitation. Prayer was healing; prayer was poetry.

I started writing poetry during my university years in the 1960s. Most of those first poems are lost; besides, very early in my development as a writer I was drawn to writing novels instead of poetic forms. If lyricism appears in my prose, it can also be said that my poems often lean toward narrative. Story and poem intermingle. It is not just my own work that does this: the early poetic epics of many cultures tell fantastic stories.

In "A Child's Christmas in New Mexico," I am the child narrator describing a Christmas morning. The poem is a song of innocence; the birth of my poetic consciousness is analogous to the birth of Jesus. Innocence is steeped in family, home, simple gifts, and joy in the day in spite of obvious poverty. Christmas means welcoming family and neighbors to the table laden with my mother's traditional Christmas dishes and desserts: homemade posole with pork, chile colorado con hamburger meat, tortillas de harina, macarones with cheese, biscochitos, empanadas, pastelitos de fruta, natillas, and sopa, a sweet bread pudding fit for the Christ Child. Poetry came in the food we ate.

Innocence doesn't last. I entered school, where my Spanish

language wasn't allowed. (Imagine stifling the voice of the budding poet!) At that time Mexican American culture and history weren't taught in the public schools. I wrote "Walt Whitman Strides the Llano of New Mexico" during the years of the Chicano movement. The Mexican American community demanded social justice, and poets far more accomplished than I were in the forefront of that civil rights struggle. Was there a poet whose voice and message could redress social wrongs? I had read Whitman, so I turned to him, believing that his spirit could vanquish oppression. His healing voice and message resonated with me. In the poem he strides across New Mexico, marching alongside Chicanos and Chicanas. Why not? His ritualistic poetry belongs to all world communities.

When I write, I cast myself into the world of the poem; I enter the time and realm of ritual. In many traditional healing ceremonies, the patient being cured enters a trancelike state, his or her injured soul seeking Truth. By being cast into the Absolute, the patient is healed, and then returns to community. By writing, reciting, or listening to a poem, we are cast out of self into Truth, and we are made spiritually stronger. All creators in the arts know this. Healing takes place when we are cast out of self into Essence, then return to participate fully in community. We are not alone when we are in our poetic trance; around us, community attends the ritual.

Two of our heroes in the early days of the Chicano movement were César Chávez and Dolores Huerta. When César died, I was moved to eulogize him. I read the poem Shelley wrote for Keats and there found enough consolation to begin my elegy. Personal grief fueled the poem, much like dancing, chanting, and drumming accompany a traditional shamanic healing ceremony. Being cast out of my personal world into the poem, I discovered that César's spirit is still with us. It still guides us. I returned to community with the poem in hand, which I hope provides both hope and catharsis for the reader.

Some will consider "The Adventures of Juan Chicaspatas" rasquache poetry, mixing my love for classical epics with the journey of two Chicano homeboys searching for their mestizo identity. In the 1970s Chicanos were rediscovering Aztlán, the ancient homeland of the Aztecs, the homeland that was also ours through our mestizo heritage. I read Aztec mythology, and from bits and pieces of knowledge gained from Aztec cosmogony, the poem evolved. Puro rasquache. The world's earliest epics offer a sense of communal or national identity, so I offer this humble poem as a small measure describing Chicano identity.

Alluding to the first lines of the *Aeneid*, Juan begins his invocation to the muse—not the classical Greek muse, but María Juana, the vatos' marijuana. So begins the semi-epic journey of Juan and Al Penco, a PG-13 poem that contains satire, humor, and sexual innuendo. Through the years, our ethnic identity acquired various labels: Mexican American, Hispanic, Latino. In the 1970s we identified as Chicanos. Writers from our community continue to describe Mexican American identity and history.

"Isis in the Heart," a love poem for my wife, is probably my favorite poem. Patricia and I enjoyed traveling to many foreign countries, but our journey to Egypt and sailing the Nile rank as unforgettable. We read Egyptian mythology, and that enhanced our visit to the fabulous archeological sites we visited. I fell in love with Isis, that most interesting ancient goddess, a curandera in her own right. If I could bring Whitman to New Mexico, I could also bring Isis and Osiris to the Río Grande. A poet must be adventurous; in poetry everything is possible.

I believe that curanderas were our first spiritual feminists. Breaking with traditions that restricted the social roles of women, curanderas took care of the physical and spiritual well-being of our community. Long before the arrival of doctors in New Mexico, people relied on these medicine women. In their curing ceremonies, curanderas most often pray to the Catholic saints, Jesus, and the Virgin Mary. I believe there is a deeper historical connection our healers have to the goddesses of the world.

In her role as healer, Isis was the mother who worked cures, protected the sick, provided good harvests, blessed matrimonies, helped women conceive, and assisted seekers in their quest for Truth. Isis opened the door to eternal life by helping the soul see the Absolute. Our curanderas work their healing ways much as Isis did millennia ago. The goddesses are living forces in our lives.

We are creatures who desire to see the Truth beyond the reality in which we live. Why are we here? Where did we come from? Where are we going? If reality is illusion, then the world is illusion, so can we ever know the underlying Truth of life? Know why the universe is here? Creativity is one path toward Truth. When creating stories or poems, we momentarily sunder the veils that blind, and the self encounters Truth.

The creative search for Truth is the subject of my novella *Jalamanta: A Message from the Desert*. The prophet Jalamanta informs his community that he has come to strip away veils of illusion and thus reveal the Truth. Also, in *Randy Lopez Goes Home*, Randy, after living in the real world, returns home to his true love, Sofia. In order for Randy to move to a higher spiritual plane, Sofia's wisdom must be revealed. Her wisdom is healing for Randy, his community, and the reader. Understanding the world of spirits that is beyond reality is the subject of my recent novel, *The Old Man's Love Story*. Many of my novels are now available as e-books through Open Road.

In my creations, I bring the world to New Mexico, so I brought Isis and Osiris to my Río Grande Valley. Our sojourn in Egypt was a fulfilling experience, and it provided me with a new, rich, and complex cast of characters. Now I had a new metaphor to guide my work. Isis sewed Osiris together after he was dismembered by Seth. In my ritualistic trance, I sew the poem together: imagination is the thread; the experiences and stories the world has given me are the flesh.

Prose or poetry, the world appears in my dreams, in my living reality, and in my work. I cast my self out of my personal world into the poetry, myths, legends, and stories of world communities, and I return healed and wiser for the experiences.

In my creative imagination the Río Grande becomes the Nile, and I see those Egyptian lovers from long ago wandering up the river. Isis and Osiris become a reflection, a way of writing about the love my wife and I shared. Long ago, the kingdoms of Upper and Lower Egypt were finally united, so in the poem the corn and chile kingdoms of New Mexico are united. The love of lovers brings unity.

Poetry unites. Poetry connects. In "Sailing to Barcelona," Patricia and I return to Spain. Sailing the Mediterranean world, we were cast out of our safe home in Albuquerque, the home we built together, into the journey, la cruzada. Upon our return, I wrote this poem of reconciliation; Patricia returned with new knowledge of the goddess Isis and renewed faith in her Tarot cards. We connected to Truth in our respective ways.

Travel is a ritual that takes us from the personal into the world community. We travel to other worlds when we read. Being lost in a poem or story is like being in love, making love, sensing the mystic in yourself, acknowledging life and death, perhaps moved by the epiphany to write a poem or a story. The ritual of reading makes time stand still, and therein we catch a glimpse of the Absolute.

There are shorter poems sprinkled through these pages, but I won't reveal their histories. Besides, each poem is now a memory of the time when it was composed. Poetry records memory. It's up to readers to experience each poem. It does help to have a guide when one reads poetry. A guide can be a good teacher who loves the world of poetry. Wise guides know the terrain of creativity; they understand that reading a poem casts the reader into its time and space. A good guide helps the reader return from that encounter with Truth to the reality of community. One must always return to community, so the healing experienced in the poem becomes a gift to others.

In my novel *The Old Man's Love Story*, the old man reflects on poetry. Some of the most beautiful poetic thoughts are not written, he tells his wife. They're lost to this world. Each one of us is constantly thinking/imagining poems, he says, but we don't always write our poetic thoughts. We are a poetic species.

The old man writes poems on scratch pads, hundreds of poems scattered around the room. All are lost. Writing the poem at the moment is what's important. His poetic thoughts float away into a universal Poetic Soul. I am that old man, notes cluttering my desk, many a poem written on bar napkins long ago, so many poems misplaced, some filed away, finally disappearing. I am thankful I was encouraged to get this collection together, or else these few poems, too, would be lost. Now, at least as they float away, they are embraced by the covers of this book, a ritualistic offering.

A World Soul of Poetry binds us together, the old man tells his wife. Our bond of love, she smiles. Yes, that poetic bond is love, the love the old man and his wife share. I think love was always poetry's original intent.

RUDOLFO ANAYA

Poems from the Río Grande

A Child's Christmas in New Mexico

Christmas morning, and a silent winter storm has swept
    across the llano, leaving the river alamos canopied
    with snow, and our llanito on this side of the river,
    en esta banda, a frozen landscape on which the
    bright sun of Christ's day glitters with the light of
    renewal. Jackrabbit tracks drift blue, a sign of life on
    our llanito. The tinkling of a bell announces the cow,
    heavy with milk, and in the chicken house
    our red rooster crows: Hosanna! Hosanna!

His call awakens me, my eyes pasted with legañas,
    my dream still visible at the foot of my bed, an image
    of three brothers, somewhere beyond the only sacred
    space I know, this hill, the llano, the river, the town
    of Santa Rosa. Dream brothers who call from foreign
    lands where fires bloom in the night to celebrate
    the birth of Christ.

I peer from beneath frozen cobijas, my first breath a feather,
    as the first breath of the Christ Child blossomed as a
    lotus of love, blooming in the cold grotto in Bethlehem.
    Warmth for Him was the breath of animals; for me it is
    the thaw that spreads from the kitchen where
    my mother's nimble fingers toast tortillas on the comal,
    a fragrant sweetness that breaks my fast. The coffee
    aroma means she has not let my father sleep late; he is
    not yet forgiven.

Kicking away the blankets I dress, shivering, and hurry to
    the kitchen to take the day's host, my mother's daily
    bread. Did the Santo Clos of the Americanos come
    last night, trailing presents? I learned his story
    at school, how he rides through the air, that magical man,
    a brujo like those who fly as owls in the stories of the
    people. I think he must be as powerful as the Santo Niño
    de Atocha, smug saint who sits at the right hand of
    la Virgen de Guadalupe on my mother's altar, the same
    santito who makes my knees ache when we pray
    evening rosaries to end the war.

I hurry, because whoever shouts "¡Mis crismes!" first gets a present.
 I rush to beat Edwina, Angie, Dolly, and Loretta.
 "¡Mis crismes!" I shout, startling my mother, who turns,
 flour-whitened hands pressing round the eucharist, tortillas
 holy enough to purify a selfish need I learned at school:
 today everybody gets a present! "Los míos," she smiles,
 perhaps testing me, for every child must have a gift
 in hand to lay at the portal del Niño Jesús.

But I have nothing to give. I have come without a present.
 My dreams, I will give her my dreams, images of golden
 fish and mermaids that swim the river of my childhood,
 Lloronas who chase me all night long, across a landscape
 even a Wise Man would not enter. I will bring an apple to
 your garden of sweet smells, I promise, looking into
 her eyes, ashamed that I have come to Bethlehem without
 a gift. She smiles, "Anda," and nods toward the sala where
 my sisters' first Christmas tree sits gilded with green and
 red construction paper chains, a yellow star hanging from
 a safety pin.

My father smiles, a wine-tortured smile, and I rush to the
 small living room, past the altar for la Virgen, where
 we pray for my brothers' safe return from a war we
 did not make. There in morning glory, Christ's tree,
 a piñón from the hills where owls keep the night,
 arrullando la luna con su whoo whooo. Today I do not
 heed the owl's cry nor the rooster's hosanna, nor the cold
 in the room. Today I tear open a red paper bag to reveal
 my mother's love: a pair of brand-new calzoncillos.
 Long johns! With a flap in the seat! When I go to the
 excusado outside, I will open the flap and stay warm.

Long after I am a grown man and no longer wear the calzoncillos
 of childhood, my heart will whisper:
 She truly loved you.

I wanted a bike, a BB gun, a cap pistol in a leather holster,
     like Hopalong Cassidy and Roy Rogers wear in the
     movies. Maybe a .22 rifle so I could shoot La Llorona
     when she chases me along the river's edge. Instead, there
     under the tree are my long johns, the white cotton
     my swaddling. The red paper crinkles like the blood of
     Christ, which I already know will be spilled the day He
     hangs on the cross at church, the helpless saints around
     Him clothed in purple. His blood is the blood of
     innocent children in the far corners of the world.

My sisters are the lucky ones. Santo Clos has filled four of
     my father's socks with Christmas candy, hard sweet
     lozenges that last and last until, teeth-crushed,
     they disappear down innocent throats, as the host
     disappears at communion, sweet and foreign tasting.
     The socks also hold nuts and oranges. A feast for
     them and calzoncillos for me. There is no Santo Clos.
     The world is a lie and innocence a dream.

"Póntelos si vas a salir," my mother calls. "Corre, pídele
     los crismes a tu tía Piedad." I take off my pants, slip
     on the calzoncillos, button the flap, and dress again.
     Maybe in the desert story of long ago, someone gave
     the Niño Jesús a pair of long johns, for a shepherd
     needs to keep warm. The animals' breath encircled the
     grotto of His birth: sheep, goats, desert burros, cows,
     the Wise Men's camels. Those men brought incense
     and myrrh, aromas not as sweet as my mother's
     posole bubbling on the stove.

So, tía Piedad is giving treats this year, and if I hurry I can
     beat my snoring sisters. I put on my jacket, grab a
     paper bag, and rush past my mother at the stove,
     stirring the atole for breakfast. My father sits like a
     fallen Wise Man, repentant, he who veered off to
     la cantina and didn't attend la misa de gallo—our
     midnight mass, where, truly, last night in that stone
     church across the river, under the sweep of snow,
     Christ was born, and nowhere else did that happen,
     except in our little town of Santa Rosa.

We were there, gathered in cold pews around my mother,
   witness to the miracle, and that is why we still carry
   el Santo Niño in our hearts.

My father slurps hot coffee, a chastised shepherd who once
   knew every blade of grass on the llano. But he didn't
   attend the miracle last night; he toasted Christ with
   cheap red wine. My mother's memory is long,
   so long she remembers the history of Puerto de Luna
   and Pastura, remembers all of the families, births,
   marriages, and deaths. Forty years later she will not
   let him forget, as she will never let him forget he sold
   our inheritance: an acre from an old land grant.

Long after I am a grown man, I will come to the knowledge
   that not every shepherd arrives at the manger, that the
   path was difficult for our fathers, and the chalice they
   raised contained not the blood of Jesús Cristo but
   their blood, blood of vaqueros who once ruled the llano
   like conquistadores. Now they walk the earth like
   broken men and work for wages. The bread they eat
   is not the eucharist, but the daily bread, tortillas
   made from hard-won fifty-pound sacks of flour put
   away for long winter days, leavened with the yeast
   of a wife's love.

Long after I am a grown man, I will know in my heart that
   the breakfast of atole, tortillas, and Jell-O cooled at the
   window was a feast, a real Christmas present from
   that Joseph and Mary who toiled in poverty in that
   cold of the world which had settled over the Pecos
   River Valley like una frezada de hielo, covering the
   dreams of la gente. The llano blizzards of my
   childhood taught us a faith as strong as the miracle of
   Christ.

Outside, I shade my eyes, for the brilliant sun of Christ shines
on a fairyland created from ice and snow. The world of
earth, toil, and sweat is transformed. The world is made
new, Christ is born in a grotto far from my llano—an
enclosure I will one day enter on my travels through
Israel—and I feel the wonder of creation, as I feel it
this morning. Today, here, I am alive! This is my first
morning on earth! I feel truth and beauty welling up from
the frozen earth!

I whistle and call Sporty, my gold-haired husky, my loyal
friend, he who walks with me in the valley of
La Llorona and el Coco, he who stays by my side in
my dark journeys down the river, where I meet more
monsters and ghosts than any child deserves. He is
my guardian spirit in my growing years. He can stand,
like Christ, against the monsters who live in the cuentos
and live in my heart. Sporty will die in a pool of blood
by don José's lake, where summer evenings I fished for tiny
perch. His spirit will roam there at night, in that llanito
we called home.

I peer across the frozen landscape, the llano, the river trees
canopied with snow, the sleeping town of Santa Rosa
across the river, celebrating Christmas Day with
Tree of Life, cross of Christ, love of family, presents
exchanged, all determined to forge from pobreza a new
day, as the solstice sun creates a new season, as
Christ is born again and again into our lives, god of
fertility, renewing the earth so spring may blossom in
the orchards of Puerto de Luna.

Later the Río Grande will become my valley, but I will
never live in it as fully as this Christmas morning.
Childhood has made me one with sun, icy earth,
birth of Christ, my dog's bark as he chases a jack-
rabbit across the frozen tundra, my llano. Run, run,
for it's a child's Christmas on the earth I know, a new
awakening, and the sting of cold in my lungs is a
baptism of fire. Run, run, for the world knows no
end, no corner, no stone left unturned, no miracle
felt as brooding deep as the birth of a child's faith.

In stories I will learn that in the northern villages of
Córdova, Peñasco, and Truchas, the abuelos come in
the night, the village men wearing masks and cracking
whips. "¡Los Abuelos!" the children cry and run to
hide. Luminarias are lit; the abuelos cry in high
falsetto. "¿Sabes tus oraciones?" they ask in the
old Spanish of the mountains. "Ju been a goot boy?"
they say in mocho, the English that creeps in like a
frog in the throat. They are not Santo Clos bringing
presents; they are spirits of the mountains who once a
year descend to frighten children into prayers and
obedience.

There are no abuelos in Santa Rosa, unless I count Narciso,
who crosses the bridge and trudges up our path, past
the juniper tree where Billy the Kid was shot.
Narciso towers like an abuelo, his thick mustache
glistening with ice, his trench coat fluttering, his
curses greeting the day, breaking the snow. He comes
to see if Papá has la cura, a drop of wine to cure
last night's binge. Narciso at the juniper tree, tree of
life, Christ's tree, on this cold, cold morning.

"Wheeet!" I whistle, and Narciso sees me, a dot on the earth,
a child seeking his crismes, gifts of pleasure, candy as
sweet as the communion host I take at church.
He waves, this abuelo, old man, town drunk, he is Christ
at the tree, for birth also forges the nails of death, and
Narciso will die years later, in a story told by me.
"¡Mis crismes!" I shout, and he hears me, because
he calls back, "¡Los míos!"

"Wheet!" I whistle again, calling Sporty from the chase,
and I turn and run to my tía Piedad's house.
Heart pounding, I knock and shout "¡Mis crismes!
¡Mis crismes!" and she answers with a pastelito de
ciruela and a few biscochitos, treats far sweeter than
pastries from those French cafes where I will one day
sit, dreaming of home and the faces that filled the
Christmas when I was truly born.

"Toma," tía Piedad says, adding a red delicious apple.
    I know she has been baking empanadas; her kitchen
    reeks of sweet dough, mincemeat, nuts. For an
    empanada, I would give away everything I own:
    my knife, my marbles, my top. But she will not be
    moved. "¡Anda, vete!" she says, and closes the door.

I run to the González home, to the Chávez home, to Fío's, adding candy
    to my bulging saco, until I can run no more and my feet
    are as frozen as last night when the mile walk to church
    was penance enough. Nochebuena. Noche de paz.
    "Silent Night" we sang at school. A song from far away we
    sang with a Spanish accent while Abel picked his nose,
    Lloyd coughed, and Tony pinched the girls in those school-
    rooms where my memory lies pasted to silent walls.

Others arrive, Benito and Pablita
    from god knows where, their truck full of
    their sad children, tío Zacarías with his battered suitcase,
    tíos y tías from Puerto de Luna, vaqueros and borregueros
    from the llano beyond the edge of the cold earth.

Later I will remember the voices of the old people as they
    gathered around the warmth of the kitchen stove.
    "No teníanos nada," they whispered. "No teníanos
    nada." For a child the nada was a universe, a bagful
    of candy, rushing back into the kitchen where Papá
    and Narciso shared a half-empty bottle of Tokay, the
    posole simmering on the butane stove, my mother's
    empanadas hidden in a bowl, my sisters rising madder
    than hell because I beat them to tía Piedad's house.

That was mis crismes, then as it is now, an innocence I
    haven't forgotten. My crismes was that warm place at the
    kitchen table, listening to the stories of the elders,
    their words describing blizzards whose cold fingers
    devoured man and beast. "En aquel año llegó una
    tempestad que cubrió las casas," Narciso intoned, and told
    the story of each family, how they survived, those who
    froze to death on the road to Vaughn, babies born in the midst
    of a storm, hundreds of sheep found strung like
    rosary beads along fences when the thaw came.

"No teníanos nada," they shrugged. But, por Dios Santo,
　　we had each other, we had familia, we had mothers
　　who could multiply tortillas and feed the multitudes
　　who came to visit on Christmas Day. Our huge pot
　　of posole never emptied, and the red chile con carne
　　tan sabroso that it lay asleep on lips and tongue,
　　awakening in my manhood years in moments of passion.
　　Yes, it was the passion of Christ being born, passion in the
　　stories they told, in my mother's food, in the apple I placed
　　on her plate.

We had each other, I repeat, as today we seek each other,
　　gathering for one glimpse of that innocence when
　　Christ and Buddha and Muhammad were born, for
　　around the world the birth of each prophet brings a
　　new awareness of God's plan, brings the clarity I felt
　　that Christmas Day, brings a temptation in the spiral
　　of knowledge. We seek each other, seek the old stories,
　　fabulous tales, the kind I never learned at school, the kind
　　writ not in books but in the memory of the old people.
　　They tilled the earth, broke bread together, battled the
　　weather, were born and died, passing like players
　　in front of my eyes.

Their struggles were epic, and that is why we write their stories.
　　They suffered in their faith, I could tell by the webs on
　　their faces, faces burned by wind and sun, lashed by storms,
　　they survived. Survival was engraved in the sound of
　　their voices. They gathered in our home to tell their
　　stories, in the hubbub of my mother's kitchen, warming me
　　with their breath on that day of my birth.
　　Lord of this earth, help me remember their faith.

In distant Sangre de Cristo villages, the people had "Los Pastores"
        and "Las Posadas," plays to draw the faithful to
        la misa de gallo. Nochebuena, noche de paz.
        We had my mother, now gone to the spirit world of the
        ancestors. There she is waiting for us, cooking huge pots
        of beans, chile colorado, papas fritas, piles of tortillas,
        and natillas for dessert. Feeding us, she renewed her faith,
        as la Virgen's milk renews the Child in the grotto.
        She kept her faith as the sky keeps its clouds on a summer
        day. She would pray until God and the saints tired and
        granted her wish, that the wars of the world would end,
        that sons would return home.

My knees still burn from those long rosaries and novenas
        she led in front of her blessed Virgen. My bones still
        shiver when I recall the Long Walk from our adobe home,
        down the path to the bridge, burrowed into coats against
        the cold, trudging through the empty streets of the town
        to the church, blessed sanctuary.

That's all we had. La nochebuena, la misa de gallo, the cry of
        mis crismes. Our first Christmas tree serenaded by
        people who came to share our simple Christmas feast.

For everyone the day was a journey to Bethlehem, a return home.
        That day I was born again in the mystery of sun, snow,
        earth, plumes of breath, icicles that dripped with the
        water of the moon as winter sun returned from its solstice home.
        That night, as I lay me down to sleep, I would think of
        the Santo Niño, falling asleep after His first day on earth,
        dreaming of us who would come later to be born
        on Christmas Day, as we are reborn cada día
        until the world's end.

Song to the Río Grande

Oh, Wild River,
my Río Grande,
how I love you!
Sweet soul,
on you we depend
now and forever.

You are the road
our fathers followed
to an enchanted land
to plant our roots.
Villages of adobe,
cities so beautiful.

Born from the snows
and summer rains,
in the Sangre de Cristo
your veins were formed.
Murmur of waters,
happily bubbling,
you flow down singing.
Splashing!
Sparkling!
Dancing!
Dressed in finery
a river stupendous!
You are the soul
of our New Mexico.

With waters breaking
from northern mountains,
you give us life
in this your valley.
Our happiness.

Thanks to the spirit
of living waters,
on you we depend
now and forever.

Canción al Río Grande

O, Río Bravo,
mi Río Grande,
¡cómo te amo!
Anima dulce,
de ti dependemos
hoy y por siempre.

Eres el camino
nuestros padres siguieron
a tierra encantada
a sembrar las raíces.
Pueblos de adobe,
ciudades muy bellas.

Naces de nieves
y lluvias de verano,
en Sangre de Cristo
se forman tus venas.
Murmullo de aguas,
burbujas alegre,
bajas cantando.
¡Salpicando!
¡Chispeando!
¡Bailando!
Vestido de gala
¡un río estupendo!
Eres el alma
de nuestro Nuevo México.

Con aguas brotando
de sierras norteñas,
tú nos das vida
en éste tu valle.
Nuestra alegría.

Gracias espíritu
de aguas vivas,
de ti dependemos
hoy y por siempre.

Cornerstones

FOR JOE SANDO

Mother Earth, you are our cornerstone in the cosmos.
Your ocean clouds anchor us to the seasons, your
mountains rise as building blocks, joining beloved earth
to sky. Rivers and wind rush, wearing away clay and sand.
This is as it should be.

Here in New Mexico, native ancestors paused to chisel
images on Earth's monoliths. Petroglyphs are the first
cornerstones of our land, sacred figures protecting the
community from floods, windstorms, earthquakes.

Chaco, Mesa Verde, Casas Grandes, rock buildings rose,
mud pueblos rose, cornerstones were laid, the people
prospered, the ceremonies were kept, the people danced.

Other people appeared on the land, carrying on tired
backs a cross, a new cornerstone to plant in the earth.
They, too, built mud pueblos and set the cornerstones of
their faith: Familia, el pueblo.

They raised churches they thought would last forever.
Timbers from the mountains, thousands of adobes placed by
brown hands. A new religion, new ceremonies and fiestas.
A web of cornerstones lacing communities together.

But even cornerstones crumble; not only weather washes
away adobe mud. Communities rise against each other, wars
follow, history intrudes, with time new people arrive
on the blessed earth, new languages sprout. Until a
desire to live in peace creates new cornerstones:
harmony, neighbor helping neighbor, understanding.

Now our cornerstone, Mother Earth, is falling apart,
crumbling under the weight of our troublesome needs.
Homes and places of worship need repair, as do our hearts.
Can the heart be a cornerstone? Can a web of hearts
become a new community that restores our Earth?
This we believe: working together, we can renovate
this place that many languages call home.

Alhucema

FOR GLORIA

Flor de semana santa
flor de pasión
alas blancas
alas de angelito
corazón amarillo.
Alhucema, alhucema
hija de tierra santa
corazón de primavera
alas blancas
recuerdas mi pasión—
Vientos calorosos
pasión, pasión . . .
Murió el profeta
días y noches de pasión.
Se levantó el hombre
de su tomba nocterna,
besó las alas
de su amada . . .
En las calles
las mujeres lloran
y se van.
Alhucema, flor de primavera,
beso tus alas blancas,
pasión de los días.
Beso los labios de mi amada,
mujer alhucema,
pasión de primavera.

Walt Whitman Strides the Llano of New Mexico

I met Walt, kind old father, on the llano,
    That expanse of land, eagles, and cactus
    Where the Mexicano met the Indio, and both
    Met the tejano, along the Río Pecos, our
    River of blood, River of Billy the Kid,
    River of Fort Sumner where the Diné suffered,
    River of the Golden Carp, god of my gods.

He came striding across the open plain,
    There where the owl calls me
    To the shrine of my birth,
    There where Ultima buried my soul-cord,
    The blood, the afterbirth, my destiny.

His beard, coarse, scraggly, warm, filled with sunlight,
    Like llano grass filled with grasshoppers,
    Protection for lizards and jackrabbits,
    Rattlesnakes, coyotes, and childhood fears.

"Buenos días, don Walt!" I called. "I have been waiting
    For you. I knew you would one day
    Leap across the Mississippi!
    Leap from Mannahatta! Leap over the Brooklyn Bridge!
    Leap over slavery! Leap over the technocrats!
    Leap over atomic waste! Leap over the violence!
    Madonna! Dead-end rappers!
    Peter Jennings and ungodly nightly news!
    Leap over your own sex!
    Leap to embrace la gente de Nuevo México!
    Leap to miracles!"

I always knew that. I dreamed that.

I knew you would one day find the Mexicanos of my land,
　　The Nuevo Mexicanos who kicked ass with our
　　Indian ancestors, kicked ass with the tejanos,
　　And finally got their ass kicked by politicians!
　　I knew you would find us Chicanos, en la pobreza,
　　Always needing change for a ride or a pint.
　　¡Pero ricos en el alma!
　　¡Ricos en nuestra cultura!
　　¡Ricos con sueños y memoria!

I kept the faith, don Walt, because I always knew
　　You could leap continents!
　　Leap over the squalor!
　　Leap over pain and suffering,
　　And the trash heap we make of our Earth!
　　Leap into my arms.

Let me nestle in your bigote, don Walt,
　　As I once nestled in my abuelo's bigote,
　　Don Liborio,
　　Patriarch of the Mares clan, padre de mi mamá.
　　Farmer from Puerto de Luna, mestizo de España y
　　México, católico y judío, moro e indio, francés,
　　Y mountain man, ¡hombre de la tierra!

Let me nestle in your bigote, don Walt,
　　Like I once nestled in the grass of the llano,
　　On summer days,
　　A child lost in the wide expanse, brother to lagarto,
　　Jackrabbit, rattlesnake, vulture, and hawk.
　　I lay sleeping in the grama grass, feeling the groan
　　Of the Earth beneath me, ¡tierra sagrada!
　　Around me, grasshoppers chuffing, mockingbird calling,
　　Meadowlark singing, owl warning, rabbit humping,
　　Flies buzzing, worms turning, vulture and hawk
　　Riding air currents,
　　Brujo spirits moving across my back and raising the hair
　　On the back of my neck,
　　Golden fish of my ponds tempting me to believe
　　In the gods of the earth, water, air, and fire.
　　¡Oriente, poniente, norte, sur, y yo!

Dark earth groaning beneath me, sperm flowing,
    Sky turning orange and red, nighthawk's dart, bat's flitter,
    The mourning call of La Llorona filling the night wind
    As the *presence of the river* stirred, called my name:
    "¡Hijo! ¡Hiiiii-jo!"

And I fled, fled for the safety of my mother's arms.

You know the locura of childhood, don Walt—
    That's why I welcome you to the llano, my llano,
    My Nuevo México! ¡Tierra sagrada! ¡Tierra sagrada!

Hold me in the safety of your arms, wise poet, old poet,
    Abuelo de todos. Your fingers stir my memory.

The high school teachers didn't believe in the magic
    Of the Chicano heart.
    They fed me palabras sin sabor
    When it was your flesh I yearned for. Your soul.
    They teased us with "O Captain! My Captain!"
    Read silently so as to arouse no passion, no tears,
    No erections, no bubbling love for poetry.

¡Qué desgracia! What a disgrace! To give my soul only
    One poem in four years when you were a universe!

¡Qué desgracia! To give us only your name, when you were
    Cosmos, and our brown faces yearned
    For the safety of your bigote, your arms!

¡Qué desgracia! That you have to leap from your grave,
    Now, in this begetting time, to kick ass with this country
    Which is so slow to learn that we are the magic in the soul!
    We are the dream of Aztlán!

¡Qué desgracia! That my parents didn't even know
    Your name! Didn't know that in your *Leaves of Grass*
    There was salvation for the child.
    I hear my mother's lament: "They gave me no education!"
    I understand my father's stupor: "They took *mi honor,
    mi orgullo, mi palabra.*"

¡Pobreza de mi gente! I strike back now! I bring you,
    Don Walt, to help gird our loins!
    ¡Este viejo es guerrillero por la gente!
    ¡Guerrillero por los pobres! ¡Los de abajo!

"Save our children now!" I shout. "Put *Leaves of Grass* in their
    Lunch boxes! In the tacos and tamales!
    Let them call him Abuelo! As I call him Abuelo!
    Chicano poets of the revolution! Let him fly with you
    As your squadrons of words fill the air over Aztlán!
    ¡Mujeres chicanas! Pull his bigote as you would tug
    At a friendly abuelo! His manhood is ours!
    Together we are One!"

¡Pobreza! Child wandering the streets of Burque!
    Broken by the splash of water, elm seed ghost,
    Lost and by winds of spring mourned,
    By La Llorona of the Río Grande mourned,
    Outcast, soul-seed, blasted by the wind of the universe,
    Soul-wind, scorched by Grandfather Sun, Lady Luna,
    Insanity, grubs scratching at broken limbs,
    Fragmented soul.

I died and was buried, and years later I awoke from the dead
    And limped up the hill where your *Leaves of Grass*
    Lay buried in library stacks.

"Chicano Child Enters University!" the papers cried.
    "Miracle Child! Strange Child! Dark Child!
    Speaks Spanish Child! Has Accent Child!
    Needs Lots of Help Child! Has No Money Child!
    Needs a Job Child! Barrio Child!
    Poor People's Child! Gente Child! Dropout Child!"

"I'll show you," I sobbed, entering the labyrinth of loneliness,
    Dark shadows of library, cold white classrooms.

You saved me, don Walt, you and my familia that held me up,
    Like a crutch holding the one-legged Man,
    Like Amor holding the lover,
    Like a kiss holding the flame of Love.

You spoke to me of your Mannahatta, working men and women,
    Miracle of democracy, freedom of the soul,
    The suffering of the Great War, the death of Lincoln,
    The lilacs' last bloom, the pantheism of the Cosmos,
    The miracle of Word.

Your words caressed my soul, soul meeting soul.
    You opened my mouth and forced me to speak!
    Like a cricket placed on a dumb tongue,
    Like the curandera's healing herbs and touch,
    Which taught me to see beauty,
    Your fingers poked and found my words!
    You drew my stories out.
    You believed in the Child of the Llano.

I fell asleep on *Leaves of Grass*, covering myself
    With your bigote, dreaming my ancestors, my healers,
    The cuentos of their past, dreams, and memories.

I fell asleep in your love, and woke to my mother's
    Tortillas on the comal, my father's cough,
    My familia's way to work, the vast love that was
    An ocean in a small house.

I woke to write my *Leaves of Llano Grass*, the cuentos
    Of the llano, ¡tierra sagrada! I thank the wise teacher
    Who said, "Dark Child, read this book!
    You are grass and to grass you shall return."

¡Gracias, don Walt! Enjoy your stay. Come again.
    Come every day. Our niños need you, as they need
    Our own poets. Maybe you'll write a poem in Spanish,
    I'll write one in Chinese. All of poetry is One.

Ismith Khan in the Jemez Mountains

SEPTEMBER 22, 1996

Ismith and Betty, on this first day
of autumn I sit and watch the sunset
on the red cliff and think of you.

Ismith Khan is a chain-smoker.
He smokes on our porch in Jemez Springs,
    and rain clouds form over the Valles Caldera.
He leaves the aroma of curry
    in our kitchen.

Pollo con curry is now famous
    in New Mexican cocinas.
Some Chicanas claim the dish came north with their
    ancestors, way back in the seventeenth century.

A beautiful lady comes with Ismith.
    Betty writes poems
    that melt in your mouth.

When Ismith and Betty came to the Jemez,
    the mountains bowed.
The majestic cliffs of the cañón shuddered.
"Éste es un hombre poderoso," the mountain said.
The aspens tremble when Ismith and Betty walk by.

I told the Chicanos del norte
    (New Mexico, that is),
    "Ese vato es mi bro."
East Indian del Caribe.
He speaks español, he writes la lengua
    de su isla.

Pollo con curry
    pica la lengua, makes you write poetry,
    makes island dreams all night long.

Betty chases peacocks in the jardín,
    collects the bright tail feathers.
    Each feather becomes a poem.
She's a ballerina de poemas y peacocks.

Te digo, Ismith y su mujer
    son gente de amor y poder.
That's why la raza calls him primo.

When they left us, the mountains cried.
Pero they left part of their alma with us.

Chant in the Blood

Now that the pyracantha blossoms have turned brown
    and their perfume has fled the path,
    something calls me to Mazatlán.

What is this tug in the blood I feel? A call to walk
    on la playa, to sit on warm sand and
    chant the mantra I once sang.

    "Madre Mar,
    Madre Tierra,
    Madre María . . . Pray for us,
        Bless the children,
        Wash away my pain."

Or do I want to sit and gaze on the Islands of the
    Deer and Pelican as I sip tequila and
    enter the god of agave visions?

Afternoons in Mazatlán. The sun sets blazing red in
    the west, and I am no more than light
    absorbed by light, myself a vision.

Frigates, birds of huge wingspan, spiral up in
    the afternoon light, so high I wonder
    if they can return to their nests in darkness.

They do not search for food so late in the day,
    they soar for the sheer joy of height,
    specks lost in luminous clouds.

It is this darkness in my blood that calls me south
    to the land of light, where bougainvillea bloom
    eternal. I fear death as much as you.

I dream of friends whose footprints cross the sand.
    They, too, dream of light beyond light,
    a southern clime for weary bones.

In her bed, strong-willed Mona lies transformed. She
has become an Amazon. Surely she will
lead us back to the playas of Mazatlán.

The darkness lifts when one writes a poem, and the
stream of light from navel to navel
draws us together, one single vision.

I hurry to Patricia, my soul no longer as heavy as
the brown pyracantha blossoms. Let us
hurry and plan for this trip south!

Call David and Mona! Call those friends who will
chant with us on the playa! Drink
tequila with us! Mazatlán calls!

"Madre Mar,
Madre Tierra,
Madre María . . . Pray for the light within
          Pray for Mona,
          Wash away the pain."

Rescoldando Chile Verde

DEDICATED TO THE SANTA ROSA CLASS OF 1956

Yo me acuerdo, que en los años pasados,
En el mes de julio, la gente de Santa
Rosa esperaba la primera cosecha de chile
Verde. Pues, munchos tenían sus jardines,
Ahí atrás de la casa, pero todos esperaban
El chile de Puerto de Luna. Pa' que te
Digo, ya sabes que es el mejor de todo
El mundo. Ask anyone from PDL.

Esperar el primer chile verde del verano
Es como esperar pegarle al lottery.
O esperar lluvia en el verano cuando el
Llano está seco y el río apenas corre.

En el invierno sí comía chile la gente,
De aquel que secaban en el sol y que se
Guardaba en un flour sack de la tienda.
Era muy sabroso, pero ya pa' la primavera
Nomás semilla quedaba en el saquito.
Hoy todos tienen freezers, y qué sabe la
Plebe de chile guisao con carne seca?

Pues allá en junio comenzaba la gente a
Soñar de chile verde. Chile verde dreams.
Se ponía uno muy mohino. Los hombres se
Iban muy enojados a sus trabajos. Pues ya
Saben, sin chile no hay amor.

En junio iba la gente a Puerto de Luna,
Izque a visitar a parientes. Pero todos
Sabían que iban a esportear las siembras
De chile. ¡Ay qué matas tan bonitas! ¡Ay
Qué siembras tan verdes! ¡Arboledas de
Manzana y durazno! En esos días el Valle
De Puerto de Luna parecía paraíso.

"Oiga, vecino, ¿cuándo hay chile?" le
Gritó mi papá a un viejito que andaba
Regando—su acequia llena de agua del
Río. Y el viejito le respondió, "Tenga
Paciencia, compadre. La mata de chile es
Como la mujer. Hay que no apurarla."

¡Seguía esperando la gente, tirando ojo al
Caminito de Puerto de Luna hasta que al
Fin! Ahí venía mi abuelo, Don Liborio,
En su carro de bestía, con calabacitas,
Y tomates, y manzanitas verdes para la
Plebe, ¡y con unos sacos de guangoche
Bien llenos de chile verde! ¡Híjola!

¡Qué gold mine! Salían las mujeres con
Sus botecitos de diez a comprarle chile.
"¡Anda!" me gritaba mi abuelo. "¡A vender
Chile o a la leña!" Descalzo, yo corría
Por las calles de la plaza, gritando,
"¡Chile verde! ¡A quince centavos el bote!"
Sometimes I tried to sell for dos reales.

Pero ya saben cómo son las comadres,
Todas eran muy taites con su feria. Pues
En esos tiempos casi no había dinero.
"Nomás diez centavos te doy por el bote."
Y tenía que venderlo por diez, porque ya
Venían otros vendedores de PDL, y las
Mujeres were going to shop and compare.

Me pasaba la tarde vendiendo chile verde.
Allá en Los Jarros la plebe con sus hondas
Me hacían la vida pesada. Yo les daba
Manzanitas verdes pa' poder pasar.
Y después el aroma del chile rescoldando
Se olía por toda la plaza, and if you had
Nosy neighbors salían oliendo. "Whatcha
Doin', neighbor?" Y le respondía uno en un
Inglés muy mocho, "No, me no doin' nada.
Jus'ta rescoldando chile." ¡Qué pendejos!

So ahí estaban las mujeres, enbocadas en
El chile, parecía fiesta, ¡todas contentas!
Rescoldar chile verde is an art, como ya
Lo saben. Hoy en día tienen los squirrel
Cages con propane, la gente muy floja.
Los comales de mi mamá solo tenían one
Setting, y te juro, no se quemaba ni un
Chile. Hoy todos tienen su George Foreman
Grill, y todavía queman dedos y chile.

Parecía que en cada casa había un tonto.
A él no lo dejaba rescoldar chile,
Porque lo quemaba. Pues, al tontito lo
Sentaba su mamá en una esquina y le daba
Un popsicle. Yo pelando chile y el tonto
Comiendo popsicles. Un día me dijo mi
Abuelo, "Hazte el tonto." Después de'so
Me sentaba con el tonto a comer popsicles.

Entonces no había blenders, todo hecho a
Mano. El sabor de las manos de mi mamá
Aperfumaba el chile guisado con carne.
Ella servía esa comida de los dioses con
Frijolitos y calabacitas y papas fritas.
Con cucharas de tortilla, comía uno hasta
Que sudaba. Hasta se caiba uno de la mesa.
Y después le daban unos torzones, que
Hasta en medianoche salía uno in a
Hurry al excusao. El "two seater" con el
Catálogo de Sears—at your service.

¿Saben lo que es estar contento en nuestra
Tierra? Es comer chile fresco que llega
En julio de PDL. Es el aroma del chile
Rescoldando. El aroma de las tortillas en
El comal. La familia junta, comiendo esas
Comidas tan sabrosas y saludables. 'Hora
Todos andan allá en el fast food, y el
Big Mac lo sirven con un chile muy fiero.
Ahí está la plebe pegada al TV. Bueno,
Yo sé que en esta vida todo cambia, pero

Récenle a Dios que nunca se acabe la
Ceremonia de rescoldar chile verde.

Y después, en el fresco de la tarde, una
Sandía de Tejas, fría en el agua de la
Noria, o un pastelito de manzana seca,
O natillas. Hijo, qué desserts tan dulces
Hacía mi mamá. Casi ya no hacen natillas
Como preparaba ella. Sweet enough to cool
El chile tan quemoso. Sí, con amor nos
Servía el dessert, aunque fuera ginger
Snaps o cinnamon rolls de la tienda.

En julio venían las lluvias, y las nubes
Del poniente se vestían con unos colores
Tan brillantes—naranjado, amarillo, y
Colorado—que en esa lomita parecía que
Estábamos en el cielo. Entonces salían
Las golondrinas del río, y los ratones
Voladores. Se ponía la gente a contar
Cuentos. La plebe jugaba kick the can.
Y luego llegaba un sueño tan dulce y
Pesado, el sueño del chile verde.

Y en la noche en ese valle, parecía que
Caiba una colcha de amor. Sí, pues cuando
Llegaban los primeros sacos de chile verde
Sentía uno un amor tan grande, amor por la
Tierra, por el chile, y amor por las
Mamacitas que preparaban la comida. Como
Dice el poeta, "Cuando hay chile verde,
God's in His heaven." Y nosotros también,
Tan contentos ahí con familia y vecinos.

Ojalá que no se acaben esas costumbres.
Yo las guardo en mi memoria, y la
Memoria es historia. Ojalá que no se
Acabe nuestra historia.

La Papa

In Spanish, potato is papa.
As in papas fritas.
Papas in a chile con carne stew.

Papa is not papá, which is father,
As in he who brings home the papas.

The papas belong to my mamá, who
Carefully peels one and rubs my
Childhood wart with the peel.
Each day I meet her for the
Ritual in the kitchen, and
Day by day the wart disappears.

The frog I picked up and
Carried for days in my pocket
Caused the wart, my papá tells me.
Don't pick up frogs.
Now go peel the papas.

"Papiar" or "hechar una papa"
Is to snub someone.
As in "Your papá is as ugly
As a papa."

The lowly papa also stings.
This is the way with words.

El Gato

God created the cat.
It arched its back, purred,
and sauntered away.

It sharpened its nails on
the apple tree,
then sat on Eve's lap.

An apple fell, red and juicy.
Eve took a bite and smiled.
The cat licked her face.

God finished the cosmos.
"I can do that," the cat
said to the snake.

The flood came, and Noah
called all the animals. The cat
booked first-class passage.

Noah's Ark bumped into land.
The cat daintily stepped out.
"I'll have to make the best
of this," it meowed.

Some people love cats.
Some people don't.
The cat doesn't care,
it loves itself.

Buddha Poem

The Buddha set out to collect a thousand lotus blossoms.
Arranged in a circle, he thought, the flowers would
reflect the beauty of the moon.
But he had not collected five before the first
began to wilt.
He worked faster, but still the blossoms faded behind
him, leaving only the memory of their fragrance
in the evening air.

Elegy on the Death of César Chávez

I weep for Adonais—he is dead!
O, weep for Adonais! though our tears
Thaw not the frost which binds so dear a head!
                                                    SHELLEY

We have wept for César until our eyes are dry,
    Dry as the fields of California that he loved so well,
        And now lie fallow.
    Dry as the orchards of Yakima, where dark buds
        Hang on trees and do not blossom.
    Dry as el Valle de Tejas, where people
        Cross their foreheads and pray for rain.

This earth he loved so well is dry and mourning.
    For César has fallen, our morning star has fallen.

The messenger came with the sad news of his death—
    O, kill the messenger and steal back the life
    Of this man who was a guide across fields of toil.
    Kill the day and stop all time, stop la muerte
    Who has robbed us of our morning star,
    That luminous light that greeted workers as they
    Gathered around dawn campfires.

Let the morning light of Quetzalcóatl and Christian saint
    Shine again. Let the wings of the Holy Ghost unfold and
    Give back the spirit it took from us in sleep.

Across the land we heard las campanas doblando:
    Ha muerto César. Ha muerto César.

How can the morning star die? we ask ourselves. How can
    This man who moved like the light of justice die?

Hijo de la Virgen de Guadalupe, hombre de la gente,
    You starved your body so we might know your spirit.

"Elegy on the Death of César Chávez" was published as a book in 2000 by
Cinco Puntos Press in El Paso, Texas. The name of César Chávez was used with
permission from the César Chávez Foundation and the UFW.

The days do carry hope, and the days do carry treason.
	O, fateful day, April 23, 1993, when our morning star
	Did not rise, and we knew that in his sleep
	César had awakened to a greater dream.
	And we, left lost on this dark, dry Earth,
	Cursed the day la muerte came to claim
	The light within his noble body.

He was a wind of change that swept over our land.
	From the San Joaquín Valley north to Sacramento,
	From northwest Yakima to el Valle de Tejas,
	From el Valle de San Luis to Midwest fields of corn,
	He loved the land, he loved la gente.

His name was a soft breeze to cool the campesino's sweat,
	A scourge on the oppressors of the poor.

Now he lies dead, and storms will rage around us.
	The dispossessed walk hopeless streets.
	Campesinos gather by roadside ditches to sleep,
	Shrouded by pesticides, unsure of tomorrow,
	Hounded by propositions that keep their children
	Uneducated in a land grown fat with greed.

	Yes, the arrogant hounds of hate
	Are loose upon this land again, and César
	Weeps in the embrace of la Virgen de Guadalupe,
	Still praying for his people.

		"Rise, mi gente, rise," he prays.
		"Rise, mi gente, rise!"

His words echo across the land, like the righteous
	Thunder of summer storms, like the call of a
	Warrior preparing for the struggle.
	I hear his voice in fields and orchards,
	In community halls, in schools, churches,
	Campesino homes, and presidential palaces.

		"Rise, mi gente, rise!"

That was his common chant. Rise and organize,
> Build the House of the Workers,
> Build the House of Justice now!
> Do not despair in violence and abuse.
> Rise together and build a new society.
> Build a new democracy, build equality,
> And build a dream for all to share.

His voice stirs me now, and I rise from my grief.
> I hear the words of the poet cry:
> "Peace, peace! He is not dead, he doth not sleep—
> He hath awakened from the dream of life."

I hear César calling for us to gather.
> I hear the call to a new Huelga.
> I hear the sounds of marching feet,
> The guitarra strums of the New Movimiento.
> Old and young, rich and poor, all move
> To build the House of Justice of César's dream!

The trumpet of righteousness calls us to battle!
> And the future opens itself like the blossom
> That is his soul, the fruit of his labor.
> He calls for us to share in the fruit.

> "He lives, he wakes—'tis Death is dead, not he;
> Mourn not for Adonais."

Do not weep for César, for he is not dead.
> He lives in the hearts of those who loved him,
> Who worked and marched and ate with him,
> And those who believed in him.

His disciples know he is not dead,
> For in the dawn we see the morning star!
> ¡El lucero de Dios!
> Light comes to illuminate the struggle,
> And bless the work yet to be done.

Throughout Aztlán we call the young to gather:
　　Rise and put aside violence and temptations.
　　Rise and be swept up by the truth of his deeds.
　　Rise not against each other, but for each other.
　　Rise against the oppressors who take your sweat
　　And labor and sell it cheap.

　　　　"Rise, mi gente, rise!"

Our César has not died!
　　He is the light of the new day.
　　He is the rain that renews parched fields.
　　He is the hope that builds the House of Justice.
　　He is with us! Here! Today!
　　Listen to his voice in the wind.
　　He is the spirit of Hope,
　　A movement building to sweep away oppression!
　　His spirit guides us in the struggle.
　　Let us join his spirit to ours!
　　Sing with me. Sing all over this land!

　　　　"Rise, mi gente, rise!
　　　　Rise, mi gente, rise!
　　　　Rise, mi gente, rise!"

Solstice, 2003

This is a day of wonder,
    holy with frost, tremulous.
    I am a silent sentry at my post,
    druid of the neighborhood which
    goes to sup without a care.

The sun sinks south by southwest, there
    to misty Machu Picchu, and in my heart
    of hearts an ancient memory stirs.

The sun stands still.
    Dread fills the evening dusk,
    the settled streets where I walk,
    pause, remembering . . .

On Machu Picchu the sun is tethered
    to the Sun Post.
    Will the rope of prayer hold?
    Or will the light slip away
    into the arms of the original god?

Prayer is all we have—and there!
    A light at the kitchen window.
    The ragged farolitos of Christmas
    glowing in a row for a child.
    With gladdened heart, I cry:
    Oh, Shaman of the Sun Post!
    Hold tight!
    Return the sun to my frozen land,
    I pray.

Vernal Equinox

FOR ANGIE

In the dazzling light of spring
the horny branches of our apricot tree
sprout innocent white blossoms.
In our backyard the
forsythia bursts Aztec yellow.

At our ramada the wind chime we bought
in Honolulu chatters like the sound of
returning geese and sandhill cranes.

Overhead, there they are!
A thin cloud in azure sky.
Ah, the flight north, the victory of spring.
We sit somnolent in the sun.
Pat's Aztec god burns us brown.
We listen to the song of the unruly birds.

This trinity—apricot flowers, wands of
forsythia yellow, geese in blue light—
stirs thoughts of Angie, she who
wandered off on ocean clouds on
that distant island.

Oh, trinity of spring, cruel and
steadfast, why do I tremble?
Where lies my faith?

In me, Nature replies. I will bloom
beyond your fears and petty desires.
I will bloom in bird and bush and
dress myself in windswept clouds.

Sister Angie, too, still blooms,
in our hearts, our memories—
Even as the Trinity of Spring awakens
the Earth again.

Spring light is all we know.

The Adventures of Juan Chicaspatas

"Arms of the women, I sing,
arms of the women I have known,
women I have left behind
as I, a proud Chicano boy, set out
to find Aztlán.
To these women I sing:
Malinche,
Madre de los mestizos,
mother of all Chicanos,
to her I returned with my trusty companion,
Al Penco.
To la Virgen de Guadalupe I sing:
may she guide me where roses grow
and light my way
so the world may know
the beauty and pride of my people.
To La Llorona I sing:
wailing woman at the water's edge,
in you I found my manhood.
To my jefita I sing
and praise her every step,
her strength, her daily work,
her love, her sacrifice,
so that I, Juan Chicaspatas,
a Chicano homeboy,
can grow into the future."

A version of this poem was published in 1985 by Arte Público Press
in Houston, Texas.

Now Al Penco cried out
and cut short my invocation.
"Hey, bro, sing also to María Juana,
diosa de los locos!"
"I sing to María Juana," I continued,
"for it was María Juana,
muse of poets,
sorceress of many minds,
who gave us the power to travel
on smoke to visit
our mother, Malinche.
Oh, let me sing!
I am inspired to sing
how Malinche declared us to be
epic heroes!
I, Juan Chicaspatas,
Chicano homeboy,
protector de las jainas,
carnal de pachucos,
primo de pintos y locos,
a plain
vato del barrio,
knighted by Malinche
to be a folk hero!"

"Hey, don't forget me, carnal,"
Al Penco cried.
Trusty Al, who used to be el penco,
but Anglicized his name
because too many angry husbands
were looking for him.

"I'm not bragging, ese," Al boasted.
"Just ask the honeys.
My record is better than
Don Juan, Cyrano y el Diablo
all rolled into one!"

"Al Penco, father of many mestizos,
may our people forgive you.
You have strengthened the race.
You, too, will become an epic hero,
and many Chicanos will call
you father."

Al Penco smiled, sleeked back his hair,
and watched the honeys of the barrio
parade their beauty.

"¡Qué cosas hace Dios!" Al sang
his favorite song.
"¡Mamasotas! ¡Buenotas! ¡Aquí 'stoy!"

"Mujeres de la vida, bonitas y fieras,
gordas y flacas,
güeras y morenitas,
altas y chaparritas,
to you we sing of our adventures.
We, your sons and brothers."

"Lovers!" Al cried. "Sons and lovers."

We loved them all.
That's how this chingadera started,
just sitting on the front
steps of the chante,
having a brew, watching the honeys
del barrio, toking and
stroking María Juana, la mera
bruja del barrio.

"I remember," Juan said, "how María
Juana came to us.
'I have been sent by Mother Malinche,'
she said.
'Arise and come with me,'
she commanded."
We went with her into the dark world,
down barrio streets,
across the land of Aztlán,
into the factories,
across the fields of workers.
We saw the people suffer.
We saw the enslavement.
"Save us from this misery,"
the people cried.
Then I knelt and prayed to Santo Menos,
patron saint of all Chicanos.
And Santo Menos blessed our journey
into the darkness.
He gave me the sword I was to carry.

On the hilt of this wooden
sword was the figure
of Santo Menos.
Carved on the blade was my name.
Juan Chicaspatas, epic hero con el
Royal Chicano Air Force. Con safos.
I was their first epic hero.

"Don't forget me, ese," Al said.
"I got made a private, a real
Soldado Razo. The women
liked my uniform. Drove
them wild."

And so, armed with the sword
of Santo Menos, we followed
María Juana into the dark labyrinth
of the past
in search of Malinche.

She held the secret of Aztlán.
She knew the truth.
Through streets of neglect
and poverty and discrimination,
we hacked our way to truth.
Deeper and deeper we went into
the Mexican labyrinth,
and at the center we found
Malinche.

"She was a good-looking mamasota,"
Al said. "Mujer india. Buenota."

Malinche, mother of all mestizos,
how beautiful you appeared
in your huipil
of green quetzal feathers.
Mother of a noble people,
Indian goddess,
Woman betrayed by Cortés,
Llorona of our legends,
at your feet we knelt
and asked for guidance.

"You have returned, hijos Chicanos,"
Malinche said and welcomed
the epic heroes from Chicanoland.

Juan bowed and said,
"We come seeking the truth of Aztlán,
the place of origin
of our Mexican ancestors,
the spiritual birthplace of
the indio,
the homeland of all Chicanos."

"Aztlán is the spiritual homeland
of the Mexicano," Malinche answered.
"Why do my Chicano sons seek the
place of origin?"

"Pues somos raza," Al Penco said.
"Puros chicaspatas. Hispanos when
we need a jale, inditos
en el corazón."

"Trusty Al has a way with words," Juan explained.
"There ain't no chicaspatas in the
thirteen colonies.
You conceived us in México, madre Malinche.
We are like the branches of a tree
which grew to the north. Now we seek
the roots. Show us that
truth,
and we will return
to our barrios and make
proud a people who have
long been oppressed."

Now it was Malinche's turn to smile.
Her Chicano sons had not forgotten her.
"It is true," she said,
"your blood flows from the original
Aztlán. I am proud to call you
my children.
But it has been many centuries
since the Chicanos remembered me.
Tell me your history. How have the
Chicanos fared in
Tejas, Nuevo México,
Arizona, Colorado,
California,
y esos otros lugares
del norte?"

"Pues, we survived," Al boasted.
"We found women in the north.
Mujeres chicaspatas,
y
aquí 'stamos!"

Juan kissed the sword of Santo Menos
and began his story.
"I sing the legends of my people.
We were told that in the beginning
there was el Chris Colón, who set out across
the Atlantic,
con sus lowriders.
Decals on their boats read:
Niña,
Pinta,
Santa María,
names of honeys they left behind.
In México the españoles found
los indios, a brown and noble
people.
The primas were brown and luscious,
and men are men.
So were begotten los Mexicanos.
Españoles, Indios de Aztlán,
Mexicanos, manitos, suromatos,
Hispanics, Mexican Americans,
pachucos, lowriders, las honeys . . .
these are the many tribes
of the Chicanos.
Old World and New World
begat the new mestizos.
My noble raza,
men and women of love and pride,
sons and daughters of
the Spanish conquistador and
Indian mothers.

My ancestors are:
Don Cacahuate, storyteller, embustero.
Don Peyote, man of magic.
Don Malas Cachas, quick to anger,
hombre de sangre pesada.
Juan Pachuco, Johnny Zoot-Suit,
vato loco, protector of the culture.
Zapata, Villa, Hidalgo,
hombres de la tierra, these,
too, are my abuelos.

Vaqueros, borregueros, obreros,
guerrilleros, científicos y
hombres de Dios.
Todos son de mi raza.
My grandmothers walked by their side:
Indias del nuevo mundo,
mujeres de bronce,
raza pura.
Hijas de Quijote,
mujeres bellas.
Doña Ten Paciencia,
who gives us courage to live day by day.
Doña María Juana, who begat
the mystics, poets, and singers.
Doña Adelantada, grandma
del middle class.
Adelitas, madres de hombres
guerrilleros, jefitas
who taught us survival.
To these women,
I sing."

"That list is getting too long, bro,"
Al Penco smiled.

"But I haven't arrived at the
philosophers, writers, men
and women of great thoughts,
the poet-kings, the heroes,"
Juan explained.

"I think she gets the point,"
Al said and smiled at Malinche.
"Take it or leave it.
The español made
la gran entrada,
what more need we say,
somos buenos gallos.
Blood is blood.
We're only human, ese.
We get lonely,
nature provides.
Keep it to the gut level, ese,
La movida, el rock and roll.
Let the people use their imagination.
Let's go to Aztlán."

Juan Chicaspatas cleared his throat.
His trusty companion knew
how to get to the point.

"Yes, Mother Malinche,
my friend is right.
We need your guidance.
Lead us to Aztlán.
Show us the homeland we seek."

"If that is your wish," Malinche answered.
"Let us join Moctezuma in
his garden.
But I warn you,
the way is dark and dangerous.
The way
to the truth is always dangerous.
Prepare for your journey!
Ready your sword!
Taste the pulque!
Drink to the gods!
Light the way, María Juana!"

Malinche's words thundered
in the dark;
the sweet aroma
of María Juana filled
the void.

"In memory of armed warriors, I sing,"
Malinche cried as they
flew into the labyrinth
to join Moctezuma in his garden.

"Pero cómo canta esta gente,"
Al Penco said as they
entered the ombligo
of history.

"To Coatlicue, mother of the gods,"
I sing. "I praise her
and ask my song be true,"
Malinche intoned.

"To become epic heroes
we must journey to the source,"
Juan shouted and clutched
his sword.
"Santo Menos be with me,
Virgen de Guadalupe guard me,"
he prayed.

He straightened his cholo shirt
and made sure his shoes
were spit-shine glassy.
He was ready to journey
to Aztlán,
ready to become a folk hero.

The clouds parted,
and they entered the garden
of Moctezuma.

"Holy moly!" Al Penco cried
when he saw where they had landed.
Before them lay the grandeur of
México-Tenochtitlan,
the glorious city of the Aztec empire.

"Look, my Chicano sons," Malinche said.
"See Moctezuma, the one called Ilhuicamina,
in his garden. Around him lies
the grandeur of his Aztec
kingdom.
This God-King commands warriors,
astronomers, seers, poets,
builders, philosophers.
His word is law in
this city of Tenochtitlan.
But tonight the great Moctezuma
cannot sleep.
A vague dream has disturbed
his godlike sleep.
Lord of the Aztecs," Malinche whispered.
"What has disturbed your sleep?"
"I had a dream," Moctezuma replied.
"I see great ships sailing
on the eastern waters.
I see bearded barbarians who
come to do me harm."

"¿Los capitanes de la Isabel?"
trusty Al whispered.

"I had a dream," the noble Moctezuma continued.
"I saw the Aztecas
leave the Seven Caves of Aztlán
to settle here in Anahuac.
Four hundred years ago
they came, bringing with them
the war god, Huitzilopochtli.

Why do I dream of my homeland,
even as the destroyers
of my people approach?"

"Oh, noble ruler of México," Malinche counseled.
"Call your priests and brujos.
Ask them to interpret
your vision."

"Thank you, Malinche of the wise counsel,"
Moctezuma replied.
"I will call my magicians.
But who walks by your side?"

"These are my sons, the Chicanos.
They are in search
of Aztlán."

"I welcome you, sons of Malinche,"
Moctezuma said. He turned to
his brujo, Cuauhcoatl,
the one called Eagle-Serpent man.
"I command you," Moctezuma said
to Eagle-Serpent man.
"Tell me of Aztlán,
and the mountain
with the seven caves
where our ancestors lived."

"Oh, noble Lord," Eagle-Serpent man answered.
"Our ancestors lived in the sacred
place, Aztlán.
Culhuacan is the mountain
so called because of its twisted peak.
Our grandfathers lived
in Chicomóztoc, place of seven caves.
It was near the sea, a paradise
of birds and fish.
Coatlicue, the mother of our war god,
still lives in the seven
caves of Aztlán Aztatlán.
When our ancestors left
Aztlán, they brought with them
her son, Huitzilopochtli,
the left-handed hummingbird,
god of war.
It is he who helped
the Aztecs conquer
all the other Mexican tribes.
He has helped us build
the empire of Tenochtitlan.
Now his mother, Coatlicue,
calls for her son."

"I understand," said Moctezuma,
he who is called Ilhuicamina.
"I will send my magicians to Aztlán.
I will send greetings to Coatlicue.
Come, my sixty brujos,
go to the mother of the gods.
You will find her on
the sacred mountain of Coatepec,
mountains of vipers.
And you, Chicano sons
of Malinche, travel with my
brujos to Aztlán, so
you may know the sacred
place of origin."

"Hey, bro, I'm not so sure I wanna go,"
Al Penco whispered to Juan.
"Look at those brujos.
Scary people."
Indeed, the brujos of Moctezuma
were a frightful lot.
Magicians of darkness,
they were the most powerful
shamans in all Tenochtitlan.

"We must go," Juan Chicaspatas said
to his trusty companion.
"To become folk heroes, we
must go to the very origin
of our raza. We must
know the truth."
And Juan accepted the fine garments
spun of gold which Moctezuma sent
as gifts to Coatlicue.
He also took many precious stones,
cacao, vanilla, sweet-smelling
flowers, and the green
feathers of a quetzal bird.

"Adiós, Mother Malinche,"
Juan waved as they set out with
the brujos.

"Ay la wacho, jefa," Al Penco said,
while wishing he could stay to
explore the boudoirs of Tenochtitlan.

They traveled to Coatepec, near Tula.
There they prepared themselves by covering
their bodies with magic powders and unguents.
There the brujos invoked dark and magical powers.
Night fell, the wind howled, copal
was burned to the ancient gods.
The gods heard the incantations of the brujos,
and turned the brujos and Juan and Al
into birds, lions, tigers, coyotes, and
other phantasmal animals that can
travel through the jungle at night.

And so in this disguise they came to Chicomóztoc.
The old inhabitants of Aztlán
came out in canoes to greet them.
They had arrived in Aztlán Aztatlán, land of Chicomóztoc.
"¡Qué locote!" Al Penco cried.
"This is going to get me a commission
in the Royal Chicano Air Force for sure!
I can really fly!"
"Contrólate, Al," Juan whispered. "¡Mira!"

The people greeted them as brujos of power
and made them welcome to Aztlán.
Coatlicue's Chief Priest appeared and
asked about the seven chiefs who long ago
had led the people from Aztlán.
When he was told the seven chiefs
had died long ago,
he was surprised,
for in Chicomóztoc
no one dies.
"And who takes care of Huitzilopochtli?"
the Chief Priest asked.

"I attend to the war god,"
Eagle-Serpent man answered.
"Now we must deliver the gifts
our noble Lord sent to the mother
of the gods, Coatlicue."

"Come with me," the Chief Priest commanded,
but even as he spoke, his magic caused the
sixty brujos to become stuck in the sand.
They could not move.
Then the Chief Priest turned to Juan and Al.
"You who are Chicanos will deliver
the gifts to our mother, Coatlicue."

They approached the cave of Coatlicue,
and the Chief Priest called to the mother of the gods:
"Ancient mother, come and speak to
these Chicano folk heroes
who come in search of truth.
They have come to reestablish
their covenant with the
earth of Aztlán.
Their ancestors were the chicaspatas
of Aztlán, and they always
did you honor."

The goddess Coatlicue emerged from her cave.
Oh, what a horrible sight to behold
was the goddess of the earth and mother
of the sun.
She was old and bent and ugly.
Her long hair was matted with dirt and grease,
her wrinkled face dark with soot.
Her clothes were dirty rags,
and about her feet snakes coiled and slithered.
Coatlicue beat her withered
breasts and cried bitterly.
Her cry and appearance made
our heroes' blood run cold.

"Pero qué chingao," Al Penco whispered,
"qué vieja tan fiera. I swear, bro,
I saw La Llorona once
when I was on la peda.
Pero esta Coatli has her beat."

Proud Juan stepped forward.
"Grandmother Coatli, tell us. ¿Qué te pasó?"

"My Chicano grandsons, folk heroes de la raza,
I will tell you my sad story.

Long ago my people left Aztlán.
They took my son, Huitzilopochtli,
with them.
I want my son returned to Aztlán.
I made a vow never to wash my face,
nor comb my hair, nor change my clothes
until he returns to Aztlán.
Tell Moctezuma I do not accept his gifts,
not until my son returns to me."
And she cried and beat her withered
breasts in anguish, and the
snakes at her feet
hissed and coiled to strike.

Imagine how shocked our folk heroes
were as they stood face to face with
the mother of the gods. Eight Aztec centuries
had passed since the Mexicanos carried
Huitzilopochtli to Tenochtitlan,
and she was still awaiting his return.

"No llores, Grandma," Al Penco said
and put his arms around the ancient goddess.

"Hers is the true love of a mother," Juan said.
"Her love is as great as patience.
She has caused time to stand still
for all the inhabitants of
Aztlán.

Eight centuries she has waited,
and now the war god must return to her.
When the españoles arrive, there
will be no one to protect
the Mexicanos.
What strange twists our history takes."

"You can't change history," Al Penco
reminded Juan. "A penco learns that real fast."

"We will deliver your message, abuelita.
But please bless my sword so I can
show the Chicanos I came to Aztlán."

Coatlicue took the wooden sword of Santo Menos,
and Juan knelt to be blessed.
"I name you folk heroes of the Chicanos,"
the goddess said.
"Go and tell your people about Aztlán.
Tell them I live. Tell them the españoles
will come and a new people will be born.
Tell them not to forget the past. Tell them
not to become like the tribes of the Anglos,
and remind them not to honor King Arthur.
Tell them their Eden and their Camelot
are in Aztlán. Their covenant is with
the earth of this world."
And she dubbed Juan and Al folk heroes,
and as she did, the wooden sword changed
into a switchblade knife.

"¡Qué locote!" Al Penco cried.

"I accept this in the name of the pachucos,
sons of Huitzilopochtli," Juan said and stood.

Their visit to Aztlán was done.
Coatlicue sent gifts to her son,
a poncho and loincloth of soft maguey,
the same as are worn by the people
of Aztlán, that Eden of the Mexicanos.

Shouting "goodbye, ay te wacho," Juan
and his trusty companion left Aztlán.
With the brujos they flew through the jungle
and returned to Tenochtitlan.
Only forty brujos returned;
twenty were lost at
a wild fiesta in a jungle village.
Even Al Penco was almost lost
as he explored the boudoirs
of the village.

So they returned to tell their story to
Moctezuma Ilhuicamina, he who was
born of a virgin.
Moctezuma listened attentively
and both he and his brother wept
openly, as men and gods
will weep when they hear
stories from their homeland.
Now grief fell upon México-Tenochtitlan.
The desire of the goddess must be fulfilled,
and so Moctezuma commanded that Huitzilopochtli
be dressed in loincloth
and poncho
and returned to Aztlán.

Oh, how sad were the people of México
as the warrior god departed.
Robbed of their strength,
bereft of their war spirit,
México would fall to the men
who came in ships
from across the sea.
How strange, indeed, are the twists
and turns of history.

"And what of Coatlicue?" Juan asked Malinche.
"How does she greet her returning son?"

"She is full of joy," Malinche answered. "Her son
is home. Every mother wishes her
son home from war. She walks forth from
her cave, she is dressed in the
most beautiful huipil, the
gifts of Moctezuma.
She is adorned with precious
necklaces and bracelets.
She is bathed in the pure water of the lake,
her hair washed with maguey roots.
She glows with beauty. In all Aztlán
there is not a more beautiful
woman."
"Have you returned, my son?" she asks
the war god.
"I have returned from war, my mother,"
Huitzilopochtli answers.
Malinche turned to Juan and Al.
"Now return to tell your story to the Chicanos,"
she said.
"Tell how you went with
the brujos of Moctezuma to
the very heart of Aztlán.
Tell how you saw the ships
come from the east,
my wedding to Cortés,
your birth.
Yes, tell how you saw the birth
of my proud raza."

There was silence, then Al Penco spoke.
"That's a heavy order, Mamá Malinche.
Time and circumstances are changing
la raza, como dice Juan.
Now las Chicanas put on blonde wigs,
the men wear three-piece suits,
the kids act like gringuitos.
Who's going to listen
to a couple of pencos like us?"

"Trusty Al may be right," Juan said.
"He knows the world. Maybe it's too
late to tell the Chicanos
their earth is the
earth of Aztlán."

"It's never too late," Malinche said sternly.
"As long as one
or two of my sons and daughters listen,
it's not too late.
History lives in the blood.
It whispers its message.
Go and tell the people to await
the return of Huitzilopochtli!
Tell them to await the return
of the Lord of Light, Quetzalcóatl.
Keep their memory in your hearts,
as you keep Cristo and
the kachinas.
History has turned and twisted,
and now a new time is being born.
Now is the time for the gods
to return to Aztlán!"

At that moment se le prendió el foco a Juan.
"Wow!" he shouted. "I see it.
I see that spirit in us!"

"¡Ajúa!" Al Penco shouted. "¡Viva la Revolución!"
¡Viva el Chicano! ¡Y vivan las jainas!"

"The gods are in you," Malinche nodded.
"Already Cristo is a poet singing
parables in the streets.
Quetzalcóatl sings his songs,
and Huitzilopochtli struggles
against injustice.
So go now, and tell the people
a new time is being born.
Remind them of the covenant
with their earth.
Speak and practice brotherhood.
You, my sons and daughters,
are the new age."

"We will go and tell this story," Juan said.
"We will return to the land
of the Chicanos, to the cities,
to the barrios, factories, homes,
to the pueblos and ranchos.
We accept the challenge to
become folk heroes,
and to fight for the people."

"Right on, bro!" Al Penco shouted.
"We can do it, ese! ¡Sí se puede!"

"First give us su bendición, Mamá Malinche,"
Juan Chicaspatas said and knelt
to be blessed.

Malinche touched the knife of Santo Menos,
and it was transformed
into the Chicano Excalibur,
a beautiful Tree of Life,
radiant and glowing with power.
All the forms of life
shimmered on the sword's edge,
the Tree of Life.

"Go, my sons," Malinche said.
"Return to the world,
return to the barrios
of your Aztlán. There
is much work to do."

And so Juan Chicaspatas and Al Penco
became folk heroes, traveling across the
Land of the Chicanos, helping those in need,
singing the songs of la raza
and reminding the people of their history
and their covenant with the earth
of Aztlán.

In This Earth

In this earth Moctezuma is resting
In this earth la Virgen de Guadalupe is resting
In this earth Cuauhtémoc is resting
In this earth the war captains are resting
In this earth La Llorona is resting
In this earth the ancestors are resting.

Bare feet dancing on earth
Awaken the resting spirits.

There is a legend that Moctezuma
Came north to la Nueva México
To speak to the kachinas he came
To speak to the war captains he came.

There is a legend that la Virgen
Came to the Américas
To bring peace she came
To bring love she came.

There is a legend that Cuauhtémoc
Resisted the destroyers of his people
That he died resisting
That he is still resisting.

There is a legend that the matachines
Are the war captains of the old tribes
Striking the earth with gourd and spear
Striking the earth they awaken the spirits.

There is a legend that La Llorona is a goddess
Crying in the streets of the Américas
She cries with fear at the deaths of the poor
She cries as witness against the earth's killers.

There is a legend that our ancestors return
When we pray and dance they return
To give us hope they return
To point the way they return.

Bare feet dancing on the earth
Awaken the resting spirits.

Let us be dancers each Day of the Living
Let our dance make sacred the flesh of the earth
Let our dance awaken the ancestral spirits
Let their memory live on this earth.

The Apotheosis of Macho on the West Mesa

MARCH 23, 1988

It was the first day of spring.
Macho awoke and rubbed his eyes.

His bones felt tired.
He was sixteen this spring,
An old age for a Dachshund.

He barked to greet the day.
He ran on the grass.
He was happy.

He bumped into the peach tree.
The bright spring flowers
Were like pink umbrellas.

Macho barked at the tree.
"Buenos días, señorita," he said.

You see, Macho is nearly blind.
He bumps into things.
He bumped into Kristan's red wagon
And said, "Excuse me."

Macho has two friends, Gypsy and Chica.
Kristan was feeding them breakfast.

"Macho, come and eat!" Kristan called.

Macho could not hear her.
He is old and deaf.
His bones hurt.
He only wants to go back to bed.

"What's the matter with Macho?"
Kristan asked her Papi.

Papi tried to explain:
"When your dog gets as old as Macho,
He cannot hear,
He cannot see,
He cannot chew.

He has to be put to sleep."

"Put to sleep?"

It was the first day of spring.
The grass was green.
The trees had blossoms
Like bright umbrellas.
A butterfly landed on Macho's nose.

Papi and Mimi and Kristan talked to Macho.

They said goodbye.
They called him a good old boy.

Chica and Gypsy said goodbye.

Macho barked happily.
These were his friends,
But he was too tired to stay awake.

Macho dreamed he was chasing a cat.
The cat got away.
Macho barked in his sleep.

Papi took Macho to the vet.
Macho was put to sleep.
Everybody was sad.

It was such a beautiful spring day.
Life was returning after the cold winter.

The earth was soft.
Papi buried Macho under his favorite tree.

Where is Macho?
"Here with us," Kristan answered,
And pointed at her heart.
"In our memories."

Remember the day he chased a cat?
He chewed my shoe.
He ran away once.
He nipped a boy's pants.

He was a good old boy.

"Remember we sang a song for Macho,"
Kristan said.

Let's sing it now!

> "Macho washo was a dog,
> He wore a big mustachio.
> When he came to visit us,
> We said:
>> Don't put your head in the washing machine,
>> Don't put your head in the washing machine.
>> Don't you *dare* put your head in the washing machine."

Kristan and Papi and Mimi laughed.
They had good memories of their dog Macho.

Kristan hugged Gypsy and Chica
And told them not to be sad.

Macho is here!

Where?

"Well," Kristan said,
"When I looked up in the sky
I saw Macho flying.
He was flapping his ears.
He looked like a beautiful black unicorn."

"A flying unicorn?"

"Yes."

And a small cloud came down from the sky.
Macho went to sleep on the cloud.
He covered himself with cloud dust.

"I'll always be with you," he said.

The cloud lifted him into the sky.

Kristan and Papi and Mimi waved goodbye.

Macho was asleep.

He was a good old boy.

Aspen Magpies

In Aspen the magpies are fat and sleek,
and their feathers are always in place.
They mind their manners, but they do
rush to fight over roadkill.

In Aspen the magpies play golf and ski.
Each wears a tux to corporate dinners.
They do their feathers at a unisex salon,
and pay with American Express.

In New Mexico the magpies are a rowdy bunch.
They spice roadkill with green chile.
They squawk in Spanglish,
cursing tourists who drive too fast.

New Mexico magpies are cousins to
Coyote, Roadrunner, and Rattlesnake.
These tricksters from the bird world
remind us that we could wind up as roadkill.

In Aspen the magpies practice trickle-down
economics: I got mine, you get yours.
Once a year they invite poor crows to
dinner, but not at their condos.

New Mexico magpies share skinny roadkill:
guts, nerves, and bones. After lunch they
tell stories and wonder what it would be
like to visit their cousins in Aspen.

Alchemy

Your kisses are the alchemy
That turns this leaden heart
Toward the brilliant morning light
As we rise to greet the sun.

And so these pounds of mere flesh
Soar with my soul,
Whose gold wings weigh toward God,
Even as I am bound by earth.

I am the pestle, you the mortar.
Heat compounds love's elements
Into synthesis, whispering, earth is God
And God is earth.

We answer the ancient question:
I can live in you,
And you in me.

This season of the dying light
Comes with a promise:
Sun will return at night's climax
And make shine our love.

We cherish and bless each new day
The light
And our coming into being.

fire consumes

flesh to flesh
bone to bone
searching for love
along the edge of the bed
seeking new meaning
from smoldering passions
of yesterday.
like the phoenix
settling into its nest
fire consumes
fire releases
whispers are born
along the edge of the bed.
she calls my name
I call hers
meeting in the middle
where fire burns.

Last Wish

When I am to my death
    most driven,
Blame me not if I go
    unshriven.

Dress me in gaudy suit &
    light the fire,
I'm done with all that
    tasted of desire.

Beware the ChupaCabra

A POEM FOR CHILDREN

Beware the ChupaCabra!
It's creeping down the street.
With eyes of fire and claws instead of feet.
It sneaks behind you I've been told.
Its breath is freezing cold.

Is it green with yellow polka dots?
Or purple with black spots?
It changes color from day to night.
To see it is a fright.

"Here comes the ChupaCabra!" Papá cried.
"Run, Juan! Run, Lupe! Run and hide."
The dogs are barking, the kids scatter.
Goats, chickens, cats all run for cover.

If you've been naughty, you'd better hide.
ChupaCabra's crawling by your side.
If it breathes on you, you turn to ice;
Everyone knows, that's not nice.

Mamá grabbed the broom and swatted the air.
The ChupaCabra ducked with flair.
"You can't hit me," the beast boomed out,
"I'll take your kids without a doubt."

"Lupe, run and hide," Juan said.
"In the closet or under the bed."
Both kids dashed to find a hiding place,
Trying to escape the ChupaCabra's face.

Too late! It's here! You can't hide!
Save your goat, your dog, your pride!
"Don't take us!" Lupe cried.
"We've been good," Juan lied.

The ChupaCabra exhaled a breath of ice.
It knew the two had not been nice.
"I know when you tell lies, indeed.
Let me remind you of your naughty deeds:

Who misbehaved at school?
Who didn't do their homework?
Who disobeyed Papá?
Who disobeyed Mamá?
Who smoked cigarettes?
Was it Juan who dared do drugs?"

Papá grew mad and shouted loud and clear,
For all the neighborhood to hear:
"My son doesn't do drugs, he's not a thug!
Get out of my sight, you ugly frog!"

But Juan confessed, "Dad, ChupaCabra's right.
I went with the gang and smoked at night.
I listened to the gang in the hood.
I'd take it all back if I could."

The ChupaCabra rose a hundred feet high,
Taller than clouds floating in the sky.
Its shadow covered the entire city.
It didn't care, it took no pity.

Its howl sounded like a roaring train.
Its cold breath fell like icy rain.
It froze the kids and froze the cat.
It froze the goat that was so fat.

Call the police!
Call the fire department!
Call 911!
Call the FBI!
Too late, the kids are frozen solid!
In blocks of ice they look so pallid!

Mamá hit ChupaCabra with a cold tortilla.
"Unfreeze my kids, you big gorilla!"
Papá squirted it with the garden hose.
"You need a bath, so here's a dose."

The monster melted into a green puddle.
It began to disappear, imagine its befuddle.
"I'll be back," it cried. "I'll come tonight!"
Papá washed it down the drain and out of sight.

"We're safe!" the kids shouted. "Thanks, Papá!
We'll behave, we promise. Thanks, Mamá!"
Would they keep their promise and be good?
Or follow the gang from the hood?

Beware the ChupaCabra!
It sells you stuff that can ruin your life.
Its claws dig deep, like a sharp knife.
Fight back, don't be afraid, be good!
Toss ChupaCabra out of your neighborhood!

Forgetting

I am forgetting the names of
My apple trees.
Is this McIntosh or Rome?
I stammer and turn to the red
And yellow delicious, old friends,
Easy to spot. I know where those
Two stand.

I know all the trees by heart
Where they stand in Jemez earth,
Their branches smooth as my
Wife's arms, supple with strength
To hold a rich harvest.
But I am forgetting the names
I gave when I planted . . .

I know the leaves, make no mistake!
I know where I pruned, cut stalk
Away so blossoms could take hold.
And . . . I know how the water
From the acequia flows, how
The mower moves around each trunk.
I know the sound of apples
Falling, as well as the buzz of bees
That come to fertilize in spring.

I know many things of this
Silence in Jemez Canyon, the
Sound of Melvin's mower, or
John's truck, Glenn's tinkering.
I know the sound and light of
Sun coming over the mesa . . .
A miracle.

Like a basket full of apples
My soul is full of sounds,
Smells, images. Each has a place
In the shelves of my heart.
I have gathered and harvested
So much over these sixty-three years.
I am as fat as autumn!

But I am forgetting the names
Of trees, not the taste that spills
Sweet on my tongue, not the feel of
Earth or fruit, not the light that
Fills my soul. No, only the names.

I am forgetting the sound of words.
I speak, and in the middle I
Forget syllables . . . so I invent
Strange new words. I smile . . .
But others watch me carefully.

I am forgetting the names
Of friends . . .

Chicano Haiku

Crazy Chicano
    zooming down the road
Blue truck loaded w/manure
      Overhead whooping cranes
      head north in a V
Do you see?

Water

MAY 1, 2007, JEMEZ SPRINGS

There is water in my soul.
Sometimes it runs so strong
I am afraid I will drown.
Acequia water sprinkles the lawn.
Moth and wasp come to drink.
In Jemez Springs the mayordomos
guard the water.
Water runs in their veins.
Water runs in the elm seeds that
fall like tiny helicopters,
Turning round & round.
They cover me like moss
covered Rip Van Winkle.
I smile at nature.
That old bitch is pure water.
She guards the water
in rock & tree & lilac blooming.
In Jemez Springs colors so pastel,
those without water in the soul
do not see them.
I am in nature.
I guess I am a poet, because
water runs in my soul.
I cannot stop it.
I dare not. I am
becoming green . . .

El Corrido de Billy the Kid

Fue una noche oscura y triste
en el pueblo de Fort Sumner,
cuando el sheriff Pat Garrett
a Billy the Kid mató,
a Billy the Kid mató.

Mil ochocientos ochenta y uno,
presente lo tengo yo,
cuando en la casa de Pedro Maxwell
nomás dos tiros le dio,
nomás dos tiros le dio.

Vuela, vuela palomita,
a los pueblos de Río Pecos,
cuéntale a las morenitas
que ya su Billy murió,
que ya su Billy murió.

¡Ay, qué cobarde el Pat Garrett,
ni chansa a Billy le dio!
En los brazos de su amada,
ahí mismo lo mató,
ahí mismo lo mató.

¡Ay, qué tristeza me da
ver a Rosita llorando,
y el pobre Billy en sus brazos,
con su sangre derramando,
con su sangre derramando.

Vuela, vuela palomita,
a los pueblos de Río Pecos,
cuéntale a las morenitas,
que ya su Billy murió,
que ya su Billy murió.

A version of this poem was published in *Billy the Kid and Other Plays* (2011) by the University of Oklahoma Press, Norman.

Isis in the Heart: A Love Poem for Patricia

FIRST MOVEMENT: THE MISSING MEMBER

Anubis narrates:
    When Isis was bitten by the asp in the Jemez Mountains,
        Osiris was beside himself.
    There were no priests of Karnak in Jemez Springs,
    no votaries of Ra or the old gods
    to draw the poison from the wound.

    What was he to do but carry Isis in his heart.

Chorus: *But what were our two lovers doing*
        in those far-flung mountains?
        The Nile is many worlds from the Río Grande.
        Nuevo México is not the land of Kemet.
        ¿Es Osiris un hijo del pueblo?
        ¿Es hijo de las naciones de las montañas de
        la Sangre de Cristo?

    En esta vida todo es posible.

        Tell us the story of Isis and Osiris,
            tell it for our time, how these two lovers
            traversed the deserts and mountains of New Mexico.
            Sing of their passion so all may know how
            Osiris carried Isis in his heart.

    Pues, you know the story: five thousand years ago, in the land
        of Kemet, Seth butchered Osiris and threw
        the fourteen pieces of the god's body into the Nile.

    Isis and her sister went crying throughout Egypt,
        searching the desert for:
        Head, Backbone, Body, Bones, Heart, Inner Organs,
        Arms, Fists, Fingers, Feet, Tongue, Eyes, Ears, and . . .

In 1998, one hundred copies of "Isis in the Heart" were issued in a
limited handbound edition published by Valley of the Kings Press
in Albuquerque, New Mexico.

Something was missing.

Yes. The member of Osiris.

Gasp: *The member of Osiris was missing?*

Yes, the principal male organ, the penis—"prick"
    in American slang—pecker, peter, pee-pee, la cosita
    to gentle Mexicana mothers . . .
    They didn't find it.

Gasp: *Didn't find it!*

No, and so our reconstituted god, minus his member,
    set out to find his missing tool—for sans member
    no future was possible,
    no broadcasting of sperm-seed.

    But where was the phallus of Osiris?

A fish swallowed it, and sank to the bottom
    of the Nile.

    A Golden Carp ate Osiris' pee-pee?
        Imagine your phallus in the flesh of fish.
        (What would Darwin say?)
        Imagine a memberless god!

Isis and Osiris searched the world over, and
    to make a long story short, they came north with
    Oñate in 1598, crossed the Chihuahua desert
    (where Raramuri priests pointed them north),
    and found themselves in the Jemez Mountains.
    Sacred mountains of the west.

(The animus of the missing member hung over
    that old volcanic cone, where many a young cholo
    had taken his Baby Doll into the foothills
    to pop her cherry in his lowrider backseat.)

    But why that mountain?

The Jemez is volcanic sister to Machu Picchu,
    thus sacred in the geography of the earth.
    (Turtle mountains rising from primeval waters.)
    Men have not yet plotted
    the coordinates of sacred sites.

There in a canyon guarded by two stone lions
    (where Alph the sacred river ran),
    near a mountain spring fed by the Nile . . .

    The Nile feeds the Jemez stream?

The waters of the earth are one.
    By the ojito sat a towering phallic stone.
    (Made smooth by countless women
    who came with unfulfilled desires to touch
    the stone and dream of children. Some to dream
    of orgasms never achieved.)
    At the foot of the phallic stone,
    by the cave of ecstasy and forgetfulness,
    they found the missing member.

        Found the missing member!
            So the fish of the Nile coughed up the phallus
            of Osiris far from home.

Osiris sighs. Five thousand years they've been searching
    for his missing member.

Isis runs with delight and takes the member in her
    delicate desert hands. She raises it to her lips
    and thanks the gods.
    "Almighty Ra, thank you."

    Ra! Ra! RaRaRa!

"Now you are whole again," Isis whispers,
    her voice a love melody in the black pines
    of the Jemez.

Again Osiris sighs. "There are no priests of Karnak
     to reattach my member," he reminds his sister.

"Never mind," the ever-positive Isis replies.
     "I am a curandera who knows the magic of love,
     potions of desert lust, profuse sweat of lovers,
     the heat of tongue and pelvic thrust . . ."

"You are my shaman of love." Osiris nods tearfully.

"With the help of Anubis and Nephthys I once sewed
     you together, my little Frankenstein. I can do it
     again. Be patient, sweet."

Osiris groans. "Patient? Five thousand years have passed
     and I haven't had a decent eja . . ."

At that moment the viper struck, fastened its fangs
     to Isis' ankle, sending darkness and weakness
     coursing through her blood.

          Brother Seth!

Yes, it is brother Seth who placed the asp
     (Diamondback Rattlesnake Nuevo Mexicanus)
     in the path!

The path of Isis is the path of La Llorona,
     a goddess of the Américas who taught us
     to weep for slain children.

The víbora bit her ankle, and its poison
     went surging to her lungs and throat.
     Pobrecita mi Isis, she could barely speak,
     she coughed all night.

Cough drops weren't enough; neither were the
     antibiotics of the médico. For this was no plain
     poison. This was the envy of Seth, five centuries
     in the brewing.

¡Envidia! ¡Envidia! ¡Envidia!
It kills people as well as goddesses.

(Envy is why Seth butchered Osiris in the
    beginning, as it was in the beginning
    and shall be even unto la Nueva México.)

"To the bathhouse," Osiris commands. "The healing
    waters of Jemez are the waters of the Nile.
    As Ultima once said, all waters are one.
    Water sucks out and dissipates the evil toxins."

At the bathhouse he asks the healing sisters,
    "What will prolong the life of Isis?"

The healing sisters: Prolong life? The question has
    been raised often enough, but never answered.
    (At least not to anyone's satisfaction.)

So this is what the play's about?

The healing sisters tend to Isis.
    One suggests a hot bath, an herbal wrap.
    Another passes a crystal over her pale body.
    A third, who knows that the energy of the spine and organs
    is the same as that of the planets,
    lays her hands on Isis to correct the flow of energy.
    But none knows the way of the priests of Karnak.

Poor Isis lies pale and trembling, her desert color gone.

*The Clinical Psychologist: This is some
    hidden anger Isis carried. Some member envy.*

*The Mother: Isis is the goddess of birth. She sewed
    Osiris together, creating the first mummy, giving
    birth to future monster movies.*

*The Sensualist: She is our sister, wailing woman of lust
    and sensuality. She found the fourteen pieces of flesh,
    so the member should be hers for gratification.*

*An Unfulfilled Woman: Women cry when the male
member is no longer useful. I know! Ask me!*

*A Gay Woman: She should've left the guy in the desert
to rot. Chi energy is clitoral energy.
Everybody knows that!*

Osiris sighs. There are too many opinions in this world.
In Karnak we had order. The order we divined is gone,
the gods have scattered each to his own tent,
the world limps to its destruction.

"I only want to know how to prolong her life!" he shouts
at the mountain. "I have wrapped her in your earth and
washed her in your waters. And still she trembles like
the desert antelope wounded by the hunter."

Love is the only cure we know.

"Love." Osiris looks at Isis. She smiles demurely.
"Yes," she replies. "I am the love of spring. If I can make
corn plants grow, I can make your member rise."

Osiris carries Isis home to their cabin by the river.
That night, the member floating between them,
they make love under the horned moon.
(The horns of Ra which hold the sun now hold the moon.)

The pale moonlight bathes Isis' pallid body.
Thoth, the moon, holds himself up as dark potential.
Friend of Osiris (poet and scribe),
he long ago took five days of light
from the sun god Ra to give birth to Osiris.

Ra has never forgiven the moon.

"If life is illusion, then the desire to prolong life
is a greater illusion," Osiris whispers in the dark.

"I made you immortal with my thread," Isis replies.
"That much I know of love. Come to me."

"Do you feel like it?" he asks.

"I took an aspirin," she replies. "I'm fine."

Indeed she is.
>   She has washed her hair in lotus oil,
>   rubbed her cheeks with cinnabar,
>   filled the room with yellow-flowering Spanish broom.

She prays to Hathor, goddess of love and beauty,
>   moon goddess, goddess who brings drought, floods,
>   fertility, and hunger.

"Oh, Aphrodite of the western world,
>   Hathor of Thebes,
>   Hathor of Heliopolis,
>   Hathor of the Sinai,
>   Hathor of Aphroditopolis,
>   Hathor of Herakleopolis,
>   Hathor of Memphis,
>   Hathor of Keset,
>   I pray to you, make me fruitful."

And sure enough, seven young women appear,
>   playing tambourines and sistrums, dressed like the
>   Matachines from Bernalillo, they fill the night
>   with their dance and gaiety.
>   They pray to San Lorenzo,
>   they pray to la Virgen de Guadalupe.

>   *A night of love for Isis and Osiris.*

Let me describe how they made love:
>   The ship of Ra has now entered the underworld.
>   The Nile lies as still as a cold slice of pizza.
>   Overhead the zodiac clatters as it sweeps around the world.
>   The millennium advances on a planet lost in space.

Facing each other, the member floating between them,
    Isis breathes on the face of Osiris.
    Her perfume of cinnabar and storax arouses him.
    Myrrh, orange blossoms, and lotus tinge
    the air of their Jemez cabin.

A breeze of amaranth caresses the Nile.
    Coconut palms blossom.
    Her breath of spring wheat is a balm
    on his old mummy scars.

His breath of barley arouses her.
    He sucks in the sweetness of honey
    and the tartness of pomegranate.
    Suddenly it is spring in the Jemez.
    Apple blossoms fill the valley with their sweetness.
    Trout leap with joy in the cold waters.

Face to face, breath on breath, the silent member
    neither stirs nor disrupts their love.
    Osiris guides his fingers along her spine,
    pushing kundalini energy up to clear the poison
    in her lungs.

She sighs, kisses his eyes, tonguing them softly.
    He sees the priests of Karnak walk in desert dust,
    reminding all, the Sun's path is life itself.
    He dreams he sees the palace in Byblos
    where his coffin was enclosed in a tamarisk tree.

He sucks the palms of her hands,
    praising the magic in her fingers,
    making pomegranates break in her heart.
    Breath of wheat and barley awakens the world.
    The earth groans and stretches.
    The horned moon covers himself with a cloud
    and seeds the earth with moon-sperm.

Isis, the midwife, sees herself at Coptos
    assisting in the births of many children,
    young women made pregnant by the god Min.
    (She dreams herself, hovering hawk, made pregnant.)

(The member between them pulses with life.
    Isis is the falcon beating her wings,
    fanning life into the lifeless Osiris.)
    Like a spring wind disseminating dandelion seeds,
    she breathes on him, breathes on the member.
    Thus the son Horus is created in the world of dream.

        This is the magic of love.
        It opens the eyes, heart, and soul of the beloved.

He caresses her silken hair. Ambergris and musk
    mix with the yellow sweetness of the Spanish broom.
    There is not a whisper between them. Only the breath,
    a desert caress of love.
    They become one destiny, one constellation,
    as they did during the centuries in their mother's womb.

(Isis falls asleep, stepping lightly unto the barge
    of Ra, releasing herself to the underworld of sleep.)

        Will she return from that dark world?

"Sleep is not death, nor anything like it," Osiris replies.
    (For he has known death, a sleep so deep
    he forgot the world. He is called Still Heart.)
    "Sleep is life. Even dismembered as I was, my fourteen
    pieces of flesh could dream.
    Death is having no faith in the seamstress.
    No faith in spring."

(Isis sleeps, holding the soft member in her goddess hands.
    A sigh on her lips. Love fulfilled.)

Osiris rises and calls the moon from his fantasies.
    "What now, ¿luna de locura? ¿Luna de amor?"

"You must go to Puye," Thoth the moon god whispers.

In the morning they rise refreshed, carry corn and squash
    as provisions, and the herbal potions.
    They cross the mountain to Puye, where ancestral
    spirits wait to point the way.

"Kamaloka, kamaloka, kamaloka," the women sing,
    praising the Holy Rishis.
    The secret of the vedas unfurls in the Jemez.

We can prolong life for the moment, say the women of
    Puye. But like el mal ojo, or the curse of a bruja,
    only he who set the snake in Isis' path can cure
    the goddess, restore the flow of blood.
    (The snake is innocent, after all, a subterfuge of Seth.
    It gets as bad a rap as the Serpent in Eden.)

"Señor de trigo," they address Osiris in archaic Spanish,
    "sin la sangre de dioses y diosas la tierra no da su bondad.
    No da maíz, calabazas, chile y frijoles."

"I must find Seth," Osiris mutters, "bring him to kiss
    the wound at Isis' ankle. Make him suck out the
    poison of his envy."

"I will go with you, Light of my Light, Passion of my
    Desire, and not only cure my sick lungs
    but find the cure that will prolong life."

       What will prolong life?

Osiris does not know; neither do the women of Puye.

The women of Puye instruct Osiris:
    "The kingdom of la Nueva México is divided,
    as were the North and South of the Nile.
    North is the kingdom of corn,
    South is the kingdom of chile.
    Unite the people and wear one crown.

Go to Española, Lord of the Earth, almond-eyed Lord,
    Dreamer of Dark Dreams. Teach the pueblos how to plow,
    raise wheat and grapevines, and make barley beer.
    Teach them music."

The women instruct Isis:
    "And you, our Lady of Desire, dark-haired, blue-eyed,
    passionate Lady. Go to Las Cruces, teach the women
    song, dance, chants to the gods, the weaving of cotton,
    perfume of lilies, how to define their eyes
    so men leave off the hunt and come to lie by them."

SECOND MOVEMENT: OSIRIS IN ESPAÑOLA

"I must leave you," Osiris whispers to Isis.
    "Who knows how many centuries may separate us,
    but I will carry you in my heart."
    He kisses her ears, and corn sprouts green
    at each precious earlobe.
    (Some pendejos will later claim this is how
    she lost her hearing, bearing the corn of renewal.
    What do critics know but self-ejaculation!
    The truth is the Southwest Wind sang in her ears,
    depositing there the gift of divination.
    She could read dreams and the ancient Tarot cards,
    the desert's legacy.)

He kisses her throat, and a spring of sweet water
    opens in the fissure of the lava rock.
    He kisses her lips, and roses bloom on barren earth.
    "I'm off to Española," he cries cheerfully.

"Cuídate, my love," Isis replies. "The road is
    full of lowriders and cholos who may not recognize
    the god of Egypt."

He kisses her eyes, and a new constellation
    swirls above Puye.

"You take care in Las Cruces. It's no Coptos, you know.
Say hello to the waitresses at El Farol,
they're angeloi in the service of mankind."

Isis packs a lonche for her love. Bean burritos.
Osiris packs his member in his backpack.
And so with a few centavos and his Visa in his pocket
he sets off for Española.
(He looks like Kokopelli descending,
his own member—the seed of all possibilities—
a hump on his back. Playing his flute to soothe
los lowriders, he descends.)

In Española the cholos, hearing there is no work
in Santa Fé, have gone there,
like migrants in search of utopia.

Lonely women open their doors to the sun god.
Each one promises she can reattach his member,
make him a virile god again.
Each is as lovely as a desert Nefertiti.

I have come to the right place, Osiris thinks.
Here I will learn how to prolong life.
Like crafty Odysseus, he finds Circe by the river.

> *Circe? Who is the bruja of this melodrama?*
> *Is it Aso, the Ethiopian sorceress? Is it she*
> *who measured Osiris while he slept, so el Seth*
> *could build the casket in which to trap him?*
> *Poor Osiris, he fell for the ploy. He trusted Seth.*
> *Stepped into the casket and it was sealed shut.*
> *The cajón del difunto was then thrown in the Nile,*
> *where it landed on the bank of the river.*
> *It was encased in the trunk of a tamarisk tree.*
> *Purple flowering tamarisk! We curse the day you*
> *came to line the banks of the Río Grande,*
> *drinking the water that once belonged to corn.*

Fools! It's not Circe. It's Mary Lou from Pojoaque!
    Practicing her art of deception as a Baby Doll!
    ¡A jaina de los vatos locos!

    Can't Osiris see through her?

Osiris is a god of fertility. He does what he must do.
    And Mary Lou has special powers. It is she who
    taught los vatos del norte to smoke mota and
    sing by the river at night.

        Arms and the man, I sing again, how our hero
            spent time in the arms of la bruja del amor,
            la Mary Lou de Pojoaque, who nightly bathed
            in the moonlight de Chimayó.

That spring Osiris, our Lord of Earth and Dreamer of
    Dark Dreams, spread his seed.
    In every valle of the Sangre de Cristo
    he taught the natives how to plow with oxen,
    to plant corn, wheat, vineyards, and brew barley beer.
    He drew water from the acequias in summer,
    harvested in el otoño.

He taught that every fiesta for a santo is a fiesta
    for an ancient god. He taught them to make drums
    from aspen and deer hide, drums that sounded like
    the thunder of the mountains.
    Drums that brought rain.

He taught santeros that tree and saint are one
    and the same.

He taught that each person is born with seven souls:
    Intelligence, Name, Heart, Shadow, Flesh, Body,
    and the ever-present Double.

And so peace and agriculture came to the Nile,
    here known as el Río Grande del Norte,
    where Mediterranean people had landed long ago
    and founded las naciones de la Sangre de Cristo.
    (The blood of Osiris is the blood of the Cristo,
    as is the blood of every man.)

In the winter he retired to Mary Lou's to eat piñón,
    lay his head on her lap, and dream dark dreams.
    The earth grew cold and bitter.
    Snow fell on the blue peaks.
    A man's wealth was measured by his pila de leña.

Peace does not last in the world of man.
    Conquerors seek peaceful valleys.
    In 1846 Seth arrives with his band of hunters and
    storms the white stone walls of Mary Lou's labyrinth.
    (Even she, who has fallen in love with Osiris and kept
    him drunk with wine that cold winter, cannot save him.)

History repeats itself.
    Keep well in mind the law of repetition.
    We live in the ancient Egyptian time.
    Their myths are ours.
    The Río Grande is the Blue Nile.
    They sought to prolong life. The soul
    returned to seek the flesh, they thought.
    Mummified flesh.
    We seek to prolong life.
    We have fallen in love with the flesh
    and believe it will last forever.

Again, Seth dis(members) Osiris, casting the fourteen—
    fourteen, half of the woman's and the moon's cycle,
    half the age of Osiris—pieces of flesh into the river.
    Flesh washes ashore on the banks of the Río Grande.
    (There at San Felipe, Santo Domingo—skip Santa Fé,
    where faith has died—Plaza Vieja, Atlixco, Padillas,
    Isleta, Belén, Socorro, etc.)

This is the promise of Osiris, that in the spring
where each piece of flesh impregnates the earth,
a tall plant of corn will rise.
(Like the member rising to the prayers of Isis.)
The vecinos of the pueblos take Osiris into their
pantheon of kachinas. The gods of Egypt become
the gods of our Land.

THIRD MOVEMENT: ISIS BY THE RIVER

In Las Cruces, the Abydos of old, Isis teaches the
women to dance, sing, write stories, weave reed
baskets, spin cotton, raise the green chile of
Mesilla. People come from all over the world
to taste the chile from Hatch.
Brown Egyptian hands with Maya blood in
their veins pick the staff of life.
Chile con frijolitos, maíz, calabacitas—
the poor eat like kings.

The pregnant Isis gathers reeds by the river.
She is the breath of the morning breeze
announcing the rising Ra, Grandfather Sun.
She is the breath of summer, corn goddess.

But the death of Osiris is the death of summer.
Isis sniffs the air. The wind blows bitter cold.
The fields of chile wither and die.
Pecans drop from ancient trees. Women cry.
She knows Osiris is dead.

She shivers as she walks by the river.
This afternoon the eye of Ra is blood red
against the western sky. It was meant to be. There
on the bank of the river lies the head of Osiris.
Black as death.

Oh, cruel world, envious men and gods!
This is the head of her husband, brother, son, lover!
Splashed with blood and dirty with the trash of the river.
Oil, sewage, arsenic, and plutonium atoms
stain the once-proud head of the god.

How can Isis keep from going mad as she cradles the
head to her ripe bosom, her round belly?
Oh, murderous Seth! False god! Envious god!
God caught in filth and matter!
God made man!
How could they sever the head of the God of Light!
God of Corn!

Isis does go mad. In black she runs screaming
up and down the river bank. Her moans and sobs are
the cold wind shrieking through bare alamos!
She fans her wings, and a tempest whistles along
the sluggish river.
(Seven scorpions run before her, seven icy
winds of winter, stinging to death the
corn and chile. Stinging to death los hijos
who drink wine and smoke mota and sing
"La vida no vale nada.")

A new story of La Llorona is added
to the many already told.
History repeats itself in its awful rush
to prolong life.

Isis washes the head of Still Heart, he who
has now descended to the underworld, land of
eternal barley, Island of Flames.
The world falls into chaos.
From Santa Rosa to Gallup, from Questa to El Paso,
nothing is spared. The temples fall,
ice and drought sear the land.
Osiris is dead.
The earth is dead.

Envidia, envidia, envidia rules!
      Envy has killed the god, killed the earth!
      Will corn and chile ever grow again
      in the valley of the Río Grande?

As Osiris had once built Isis a chante of adobe—
      with vigas from the forest, latillas de aspen,
      un portal para las tardes de verano, un jardín
      con maíz, calabacitas y chile, hollyhocks along
      the border, geraniums blooming in coffee cans—
      so now Isis will bury the head of Osiris by the
      river and build a temple in Abydos, the city
      called Las Cruces by the Españoles.
      Mourners arrive to sing, drink, and
      eat at the velorio de Osiris.
      Mariachis sing throughout the night.
      "Mi'jo, Mi'jo," the women cry.
      Poems to Osiris are recited, a great book fair
      is held, and the name of the god becomes many.

Isis becomes tough like a man, and wanders north.
      Anubis and Nephthys her sister walk at her side.

      But the land is dead, the wind cold and bitter.
      You cannot end the story here!

My heart is heavy. What is there left to say?

      Why, you promised to reveal how to prolong life!
      That's what this was all about!
      Isn't it?

The story is told in many ways. Parts of it are lost
      in ancient history.

      The hell with the story! We listened because we
      thought we would learn to prolong life!
      Cough it up, you bastard! Charlatan!

The story prolongs life. That's all we know.
    Each telling is a renewal.

        There's got to be more! You're hiding something!
            You're no poet!
            Son of Seth! Anubis! Jackal-headed god!
            You're an imposter!

    (Anubis strips away the mask of the jackal-headed
        god of the underworld.)

        Oh, my god. It's not Anubis!

I am Coyote! Trickster of the Río Grande!
    ¡Hijo de Seth! ¡Hijo de Osiris!
    Isis is my mother! Nephthys is my mother!
    The world was always incestuous!
    The old gods were incestuous!
    Anubis is my primo! ¡Mi compa!
    He's Egyptian, I'm puro Nuevo Mexicano!

        Coyote, playing tricks, writing poems, telling
            stories, seducing women. How can we trust
            you to tell the story of our wandering lovers?

Pues, I'm all you've got. I am the son of Isis and Osiris.

        Very well, then, go on.

Happy is our Río Grande! En el norte the corn of
    the pueblos, en el sur the chile of Hatch.
    Thus the two kingdoms of our Nile are joined.
    One more kachina is born from the primeval water,
    from that spring in Colorado
    (land of Red Flames)
    pure Rocky Mountain spring water to feed the river.
    The new spirit wears a crown of corn and chile.

        Osiris has joined the kingdoms of la Nueva México.
            What of Isis?

Dressed in black and howling like La Llorona,
    Isis will stir up spring winds as she moves north.
    In Las Cruces a corn plant will grow from
    the head of Osiris.
    In every pueblo along the Río Grande,
    corn will sprout as spring returns.

> *But Osiris is dead! He didn't heal Isis!*
> *He didn't learn to prolong life!*

A god can never die, for he lives in the heart,
    in the memory of spring.
    He will be born again in corn, barley, wheat,
    calabacitas, chile, and apple blossoms.

> *What of Isis?*

She does not die. She comes in spring, ever searching
    for the member of Osiris. In the holy waters of the
    river swim the golden carp, flesh made fish.
    Isis seeds the earth with blood and flesh.
    She is our Llorona of summer crying in the
    breeze that caresses the river.

She teaches her son Horus the ways of the father,
    as Osiris once taught Horus
    the seeds of possibility,
    the scales of balance,
    and knowing of two ways.

> *Ah, Horus is the new Osiris. Son of Isis,*
> *it is he who will now struggle against Seth.*
> *One final question.*

I know, I know. You ask how to prolong life?
I'll tell you: Add a little more life.

    Ah, you trickster! We fell for that one.

We lay the seed of love in the dark of night,
    in the dark of earth.
We dream of spring, we dream of planting.
We grow corn, chile, the fruits of the earth.
We tell the stories of the ancient gods
and how they came to the Río Grande
to teach the eternal path.

    (Coyote bows.)

    Amen. Amen-Ra. Amen.

Sailing to Barcelona

This is no country for old men. The prayers for the solstice sun
and Cristo are done. Should we grow fat eating piñón and
empanadas? Should we cruise the mall for bargains?
Patricia, my Isis who dreams of Africa, has booked passage
on a ship sailing for Barcelona.
  So we're off to answer the call
  of one more adventure.

Cruising is in our blood. Ask the lowriders from Española,
or those who ply Burque's Central on summer nights
when the blood will not sleep. We leave our old compadres
behind, arguing Clinton's sex life and Y2K.
For us it's the call of the sea, a distant muezzin call,
  a desire not to vegetate
  in our autumn's keep.

My muses are my viejitos, for them I sail to Barcelona.
Their history flowed from the wine-dark Mediterranean to
the kingdom de la Nueva México. For them I seek new
revelations of the past, leaving behind a warm bed,
compadres with frozen bigotes, comadres complaining of arthritis.
  For them I cruise
  into my ancient history.

The friendly skies have made us all a Quetzalcóatl,
a plumed serpent leaping across the Atlantic to touch once
again the port of Lisboa. Here on the bank of the Tagus
they glorify Vasco de Gama and Magalhães, old men who
sailed serpent seas into a wine-dark sun.
  A portent of the blood to be spilled,
  the same blood sealed in me.

"This is no country for old men," they complained to solemn
wives. "The earth is round, not a flat tortilla."
They dreamed of a passage to India, gold and glitter. In the
Américas the natives dreamed a holocaust. Moctezuma sent
his priests to the eastern shore, thinking men were gods.
  The round earth's promise
  also held a curse.

It is December 31. A full moon graces Lisbon. Desire is a
movement in the heart. Desire moves history. Five hundred
years ago, men dove into the restless sea, the Américas a
fever in their blood. I shiver. What will the natives suffer
when they meet men crazed with desire?

    Civilizations buckle.

    Have I set sail to do penance?

The boulevards of Lisbon are empty; 1999 has arrived with
barely a throb. Our good ship sets sail, past the Cristo on the hill.
He blessed the sailors who went to meet our Quetzalcóatl.
This is the paradox I must unravel. I feel like a Jew,
I look like an Arab, I am a pilgrim to a Christian shrine.

    I am a shaman
    of all religions.

Christ blesses our crucero, the cruising toward African latitudes.
I smell my blood in the sea froth. La cruzada, a cross I bear.
I come to make peace with my ancestors, abuelos whose rape
bore fruit, la raza cósmica. If I am witness to history,
am I its judge? I am five hundred years old, sailing into Cádiz.

    I claim Iberia
    for the Chicanos!

I am Cadí of Moors, fallen from grace. Old Jew expelled from
Spain. The names of conquerors are curses in the History of
Native America. We are children of that Holocaust! Desire is
a worm in the heart, a hot throb that fills the sails of every man.
Old men sailing from Cádiz

    sowed destruction and
    toppled the Aztec world.

Isis does not know the many languages of Iberia. I speak
New Mexican Spanish, a manito language good enough to get us
to Sevilla, city of Archives of the Américas. We are a small
bundle of desires, traveling upriver to sit in the sun by the
cathedral. Isis, goddess of journeys, has come seeking

    the flesh of Osiris.

    African desires fill her heart.

Life is short. He who does not desire dies an unheroic death.
Old men! Let us make one more adventure of this crossing!
Do not doubt the flesh and its desires when you sail to Barcelona!
Unravel the weight of history! Rage, rage against the dying light!
Find God in your hearts!
    Sea light reveals many truths
    to philosophers and old men.

In the name of God, the Compassionate, the Merciful. Thus
begins each chapter of the Koran. I am a holy man in search
of the truth, in search of the gardens of bliss.
Is Barcelona my Eden? Is sunlit Barcelona heaven's gate?
On the sixth day we leave Cádiz, searching south along
    the phosphorous sea for Tangier.
    A night journey of dreams.

In the dappled dawn, the hills of Tangier rise from ancient sleep.
Muezzin calls stir away night's confusing dreams.
Coyote appears to tell me my garden of bliss is my apple
orchard in Jemez Springs, the river at spring rush,
the acequias full of water from my holy mountain.
    Why leave the sacred circle?
    Coyote whispers, "Home is heaven."

Old men dream of a home to rest their bones. God calls in
many tongues. Here, for a few days, I am Muslim. A sheik
from Burque. Why not? The bloods of the Mediterranean
whisper in Nuevo Mexicano hearts. Old men dream of
spangled women attending the pains they feel in the heart
    when night falls on phosphorous seas,
    far from native soil.

In the month of Ramadan we sail into Tangier. Old men fast
from food and wives. My guide into the Kasbah tells me a man
who believes is promised his own castle in heaven, with
heavenly women and criadas to serve him. It's a man's world.
The dark eyes of these longing latitudes seduce me. On the hill
    Medina sits like a queen.
    I am full of desire.

The slopping of the sea grows still in this aquamarine harbor.
The sea is like that. Deceiving colors that hurt the eyes of this
desert rat. The ship disgorges passengers to the bazaar below.
Isis buys a mirror of reflections. On the deck
the women come and go, speaking of bargains.
 I buy a vest and visit
 with the old men, my abuelos.

An eighty-year-old man is my guide. He talks of the Koran
while I sip mint tea. We speak in Spanish in the world of
many languages. He guides us through the Kasbah, a Mercado
to beat all mercados. Here, pressed by people, exotic foods,
pesky vendors, the dark eyes of women, I am home.
 I have arrived! When I die,
 many women will attend me. Angels?

The sea strait is one world. From the coast of Tangier
we can see Cádiz. There, says my guide, Nelson got his.
Billowing sails flutter, and the cannons roar as the Battle of
Trafalgar plays before my eyes. Nelson falls, "Kismet" on his lips.
Fate. The fate of England can be read
 in bloody waters.
 HMS *Victory* delivers the corpse.

Día de los Reyes Magos. The moon wanes on a burnt sea.
Of all the cheap gin joints in the world: Casablanca. Rick's Bar
is a façade. My reality is a façade. Believe in One God.
Pray to God. Give alms. Observe Ramadan. Visit Mecca.
Muslim principles tug at my heart, reminding me that
 obedience paves the path.
 How far have I strayed?

My camera cannot hold the mosque of Hassan II, but I will
engrave its beauty in my magnetic heart. Then, it's on to the
Straits of Gibraltar, Pillars of Hercules. Here the eastern world
crosses west, Europe meets Africa. The Rock rises, fog-shrouded;
the Barbary apes teach that sloth pays.
 I take a small piece of limestone
 for my home altar.

Gibraltar come from "Gibel Tarik," an Arab abuelo who took
the Rock from the Spanish. Centuries before, Neanderthal man
stood here. Cave emotions still haunt Europe's edges.
The wars of history awarded Gibraltar to the English,
and so it is. It's much too regulated for my taste.
>So on to Málaga, I say,
>sailing the briny sea. Sea of myths.

The Costa del Sol is sunlit. Isis and I ride a gypsy's carriage
through town. I tell Antonio I am a cousin from the New World.
"Hear ye, hear ye, Chicano Primo is in town."
Isis shops at the Corte Inglés. Gaggles of shoppers, seeking rebajas
after Día de los Reyes Magos. Spain is rich! Spain is drunk!
>La Alameda reminds me
>of Las Ramblas de Barcelona.

Gris el mar. Gris el cielo. Gris los hombres de la tierra.
Once again the tides of life cough us up on the shores of Almería.
Years ago we loitered here. I remember the hot breezes
from Africa sweeping across the playa. We escaped
to Granada, its Alhambra and Generalife. Gardens of bliss.
>As we leave, dolphins cavort
>in the ship's splash.

We have sailed this sea before. From Piraeus across to Ephesus,
to Istanbul. Sailing to Byzantium, a country of old men.
Hagia Sophia looms florescent in my memory. Tonight
the salt sea washes in my blood. Starboard lies Mallorca,
Miranda's magic isle. I dream of home, Nuevo México,
>a country where we do not know
>the Spanish word for "oar."

Why this disenchantment? We have come to Mallorca,
the dream island. Is it that I am an old man and I tire of
foreign harbors? My bones chill. I dream of home and Kristan.
Should old men go out to sea? I, a landlocked Chicano?
What madness has driven us to this distant island?
>I am no Caliban!
>I miss my electric blanket!

I dream of pruning my apple trees. I hear the water of the
acequia burst loose their song of spring. Jemez Springs calls.
Isis, too, is not engaged. Perhaps she dreams of the Nile,
our Río Grande, and the sun rising over the Sandias. Do we
need to stand on Tibidabo and claim the world as ours?

> Why not retire to our garden
> and read good books?

Adiós, Palma de Mallorca; hello, Mahón. A Hollywood set.
The sea wall is lined with cute cafes where summer tourists
will take their tapas: beer, olives, sardines, antojitos. This is
a peaceful harbor for tired travelers. The narrow streets
are packed. Old men and women gossip, speaking Catalán,

> glyphs that engrave my heart.
> ¡Ay, mi Barcelona!

Sunlit Barcelona! Queen of the Mediterranean! Capital of a
world that stretches from Byzantium to Tangier! Again we dock in
your safe harbor, and with open arms you receive us. Barcelona,
you are the whore of my dreams, an amazon bustling with commerce.
You spread your indolent legs along the coastline,

> proud and ripe
> with cries for independence!

Business capital muscled fat with wealth and poetry. You draw
men from León, Andalucía, and Galicia to work your streets.
Spain seeks its fortune in Barcelona. Brussels becomes
your suburb, Paris a stepsister. Madrid frets while
you grow in power. You have learned the lesson of history:

> To grow strong, one does not separate,
> one incorporates.

Sunbathed Barcelona, your symbol is a golden bull rising from the
sea, Europa on its back. I dreamed of you on phosphorous seas.
I am a Mexican Odysseus returning home. I will plant
my Chicano flag at the foot of Colón's statue.
The ancient, dark history is done. I bring forgiveness.

> Will you receive this son
> of Mediterranean ancestors?

Isis and I hurry to my goal. There is only one: to stand
in the presence of La Sagrada Familia, to honor Gaudí's mad
genius, artist who makes the earth rise in spires to heaven.
Here, I know imagination is my god, Gaudí's god. Here,
my gardens of bliss. This is our third visit, and always
    we return to this sacred spot,
    center of a billowing world.

I know this pond as I know the flow of water in my orchard.
Isis and I sit in the park, contemplating genius, dreaming of home.
The sun sets over the gnome's cathedral and calls us home.
Behind us, old men play petanca, enjoying the day and
comradeship that God has granted. Here, God is a word for
    the duende in our hearts,
    the locura that creates.

The sycamores of Ramblas stand leafless. The sun blooms in
the flower stands. We walk the thin streets of Barri Gotic and
feel at home. We will retire to Barcelona. I will play petanca
under the shadow of la Sagrada Familia. Isis will sell flowers
from a stand in Ramblas. In the dusk
    we will walk through Gothic streets,
    full of the moon's desire.

Our walk ends at the statue of Colón. My flag has pierced
his toe. Blood clots the ground. He points out to sea,
the harsh Atlantic. Is he expelling me, or have I made my peace?
I have sought my ancient roots in all the languages of the world.
Now I return home, the millennium's promise is there.
    La Nueva México
    is my garden of bliss.

¡Adiós, Barcelona! Si Dios es servido, I may yet touch your
shores once more. For now you are engraved in my heart,
in this poem of praise. Adiós, abuelos del medio mar.
Your memories stay in my blood. Sailing is not easy for a man
from the desert. But my spirit is strong and willing, and
    there is always one more poem
    to shape the future's path.

ALSO BY RUDOLFO ANAYA

Bless Me, Ultima
Heart of Aztlan
Tortuga
The Silence of the Llano
The Legend of La Llorona
The Adventures of Juan Chicaspatas
A Chicano in China
Lord of the Dawn: The Legend of Quetzalcóatl
Alburquerque
The Anaya Reader
Zia Summer
Jalamanta: A Message from the Desert
Rio Grande Fall
Shaman Winter
Serafina's Stories
Jemez Spring
Curse of the ChupaCabra
The Man Who Could Fly and Other Stories
ChupaCabra and the Roswell UFO
The Essays
Randy Lopez Goes Home
Billy the Kid and Other Plays
The Old Man's Love Story

CHILDREN'S BOOKS

The Farolitos of Christmas
Farolitos for Abuelo
My Land Sings: Stories from the Rio Grande
Elegy on the Death of César Chávez
Roadrunner's Dance
The Santero's Miracle
The First Tortilla
Juan and the Jackalope
La Llorona, the Crying Woman
How Hollyhocks Came to New Mexico
How Chile Came to New Mexico